International Menus
for the Globetrotter

Library of Congress Cataloging-in-Publication Data

Freely, Dolores
    International menus for the globetrotter /Dolores Freely
İstanbul: Çitlembik Publications, 2010.
209 p: ill.; 14x21 cm.
ISBN: 978-9944-424-74-5

1.Cookery, International. 2.Cookery.

I.Title

LC:TX725.A1
DC:641.59

Illustrated by: Kimber Longstreth
Cover design & Layout: Çiğdem Dilbaz

Printed at Ayhan Matbaası
Mahmutbey Mah. Deve Kaldırım Cad.
Gelincik Sok. No: 6 Kat: 3
Bağcılar Istanbul, Turkey
Tel: +90 212 445 32 38

Çitlembik Publications
Şehbender Sokak 18/4 Asmalımescit
Tünel 34430 Istanbul / Turkey
Tel: +90 212 292 30 32 / 252 31 63
Fax: +90 212 293 34 66
www.citlembik.com.tr / kitap@citlembik.com.tr

Nettleberry LLC
44030 123rd St.
Eden, South Dakota 57232
www.nettleberry.com

International Menus
for the Globetrotter

DOLORES FREELY

Çitlembik Publications 170

This book is dedicated to my family, John, Maureen, Eileen and Brendan, who for many years have been my willing associates in eating everything I cooked for them. Also, I wish to dedicate this book to my sister Flossy and particularly to my father Harry Stanley who inspired me to love cooking at an early age.

Contents

8

Off-Continent Menus

Asian Menus

Acknowledgement

The original version of this book was the brilliant idea
of Yelda Turedi and I wish to thank her for her
support and for her painstaking work in translating
the original manuscript into Turkish.

I would also like to thank Kimber Longstreth for
allowing me to use his beautiful drawings in this book.

Introduction

As a child growing up in Brooklyn in the 1930s and 1940s I always watched in fascination when my father cooked for us on Sundays. He was known for his perfect roasts, and his pancakes were the best in the world. He treated everything he touched with the greatest of care, and when I began to cook for my own family in the 1950s, I was careful to follow his example. But I was always looking for new ideas, too. As there weren't many cookbooks to choose from in those days, I relied heavily on *The Joy of Cooking* and casserole recipes from friends, until one day when I went to the University Bookshop in Princeton, New Jersey and came across a small cookbook of French regional cooking with recipes and photographs of France on every page. This was the beginning of a new kind of cooking for me and my family. I would cook beautiful dishes from the towns and cities I dreamed of visiting one day. When we sat down to dinner, it was as if we had already arrived.

In 1960 my husband was awarded a PhD in Physics and almost immediately was offered a position at Robert College in Istanbul. So France had to wait. Needless to say, I have never regretted our decision to move our family to Turkey. A whole new cuisine awaited us.

Our first apartment was on the hill next to the college gate, and from its enormous balcony we looked out over the village of Bebek. I can still remember our first shopping trip there. Armed with string bags we were off to find tonight's supper. With the baby in his stroller and our two girls on either side of me, we set off down the hill and along the shore of the Bosphorus. Just before we reached the village proper, we saw fishermen selling their freshly-caught fish, which they displayed on the cobblestones right in front of us. They were certainly beautiful and gleaming, but I wasn't sure about how to cook them.

Once I had promised myself to find out more about the local fish, we moved on to discover an open-air shop with the most beautiful display of fruits and vegetables I had ever seen. Almost everything was familiar, so we stepped right in and ordered all our favourites. Next we went into a butcher shop, where almost nothing was familiar. When the smiling butcher opened up his large steel refrigerator doors, the hanging lambs and the great carcasses of cows were the only objects we could identify. Settling on some ground beef, we promised to come back. Our next stop was a small grocery store that stocked most of the things on our list. Oddly, there was no coffee for sale at that time, but there was plenty of tea. We kept walking to the end of the village and found the bakery where we bought a large loaf of white bread called *francala*. On the way home the children were rewarded with a pudding at Özsüt, a pudding shop that was, as we would later discover, famous throughout the city.

The next evening we decided to go to a local restaurant. The only Turkish food we had heard of was *shish kebab,* so when we took our table overlooking Bebek Bay at the Yeni Güneş, that's what we ordered. The restaurant was full, and all around us there were waiters carrying huge trays with what looked to be an endless array of delicious-looking food served in small plates, as we looked down at our meagre plates of *shish kebab.* How sorry we were not to know how to order them! But we soon learned, and that was when we began to feel that we truly belonged.

We had originally planned to stay in Istanbul just three years, but we fell in love with the city, its people, and its food. We enjoyed the many trips we took through Anatolia, the Mediterranean, and - last but not least - France. It was not until 1977 that we decided, with great reluctance, that the time had come to leave. After two years in Athens, we returned to the US, settling in Boston. Here we found ourselves surrounded by many of our dearest friends from Istanbul. One of them was Ann Couch, with whom I'd shared a job in Istanbul. I already knew her to be magnificent cook and a most generous hostess, but now I could also enjoy her cookbook library, go on excursions with her to the most interesting restaurants and food shops of the city, and plan menus for our next get-together. Entertainment became a major part of my life.

Sometimes I would prepare a Turkish meal and we would pretend we were on the Bosphorus again, so it was always in our fate, perhaps, to return to Istanbul. This we did in 1988. With the exception of one year in London and two in Venice, we have been here ever since. Though our home today is about the same size as the balcony of that first apartment with its magnificent view of Bebek Bay, it is still large enough for parties. What I still enjoy most is sitting down a few days beforehand to imagine what to cook, and how much fun we'll have when we're all seated around the table.

I never imagined I would write a cookbook, though I had written down quite a few of my recipes to give to my children. Then one day a friend pointed out to me that I might inspire and encourage others just embarking on their cooking adventures. What follows is my life in food. Each recipe brings back memories of family reunions and dinner parties full of laughter. I hope they will go on to do the same for you.

DOLORES FREELY

Equipment

Iwould like to recommend that you have at your disposal several kitchen machines. If at all possible get yourself a food processor as there is nothing else as fast and efficient that can perform almost every task immediately. (For years, before I had a food processor, I used a standing electric blender. I was able to use this to make many things that I use the food processor for today.) Do be careful when buying a food processor. You should purchase a reliable brand from a company that produces quality products. The machines should be heavy and look strong. Today there are other smaller devices that are also handy for chopping and blending. Buy the kind or kinds that best suit your own cooking styles

A microwave is also a time saving device that you will enjoy. I put my microwave to good use for melting, making sauces, and turning out delicious pilaf, perfectly cooked vegetables and fish filets. I have included several microwave recipes in this cookbook for your interest.

An electric mixer, either hand or the large counter type, makes your work easier. A hand blender makes a big difference when you puree, either soups or sauces. These machines can make your time in the kitchen a pleasure. A mixer, both the large stationary kind and the hand held mixer are essential for making light and delicious puree potatoes.

Whatever machines you possess please keep them out on the

counter of your kitchen and use them every day. If you put them away in the cupboard you will never use them. Have them handy.

If you use a wok for Asian cooking, buy the heaviest one you can find. Try, if you can, to find one made of iron or part iron. It should weigh at least a kilo or more. Very high heat is used when cooking in a wok and the lighter pans will not allow you to heat the oil properly before adding the food.

Finally I would like to say that in some of the menus I have mentioned more than one entrée. I've done this so that you may have a choice of which one you would rather cook.

Hints

FRESH GINGER: One large piece of ginger should last a long time. There are various ways to keep it fresh. I was told by a Chinese woman that she keeps her ginger in a flower pot covered with earth. The ginger apparently keeps indefinitely that way. My method is to cut the ginger into roughly 2 or 3 cm (1 inch) pieces, put it in a nice plastic bag, preferably zip-locked, and put it in the freezer. When ready to use, choose the size you need and let it sit on the counter for five or so minutes. At this point you may easily peel the ginger and in a few more minutes you can easily cut into small pieces. If I expect to use the ginger within a week or two I then place the ginger in a zip-lock bag in the refrigerator. My daughter likes to cut and peel the fresh ginger and then keep it in a jar covered with a sherry type wine. You may choose any of these methods or invent your own.

BROTH: If I don't have a lot of time I use bouillon cubes, either chicken, beef or vegetable. Keep in mind that the cubes are salty. (See the section on broths and drinks at the end of this introduction.) .

SMASHED GARLIC: I use a rubber hammer to smash the garlic. I have found that this is a quick way to peel and dice the garlic.

BLANCHED ALMONDS: Several of my recipes call for blanched almonds. Here is how to blanch these nuts: Place the almonds in a bowl and barely cover with boiling water. Allow them to soak for a very short time—no more than one minute. Drain, rinse well and slip the skins off.

TO CLEAN AN ELECTRIC BLENDER OR FOOD PROCESSOR: After you have used the blender or processor, rinse out and then add several cups of water with a drop or two of detergent. Place on the machine and let it run for about a minute. Rinse out and drain.

MASHED POTATOES: One should never put cooked potatoes in the food processor or blender, because the potatoes become glue-like and heavy. The best way to make fluffy potatoes is to use an electric mixer or potato masher.

SPICES: Keep all of you spices together for easy access. Try keeping them on a kitchen shelf, a kitchen drawer, or a box that can be moved close to the stove when necessary. It's better to start out with buying your spices in jars. This way they keep fresher and can easily be filled from envelopes when you need more.

CELERY (*SAP KEREVIZ*) or (*AMERIKAN KEREVIZ*): I'm afraid there is no shortcut when it comes to removing the stings from each rib of celery. One must do each rib and with a knife and starting at the top work down from top to bottom to remove the strings.

Broth Recipes

Chicken Broth

Ingredients:

1 chicken, either in
  pieces or whole
1 onion, diced
1 carrot, sliced
3 ribs of celery, diced
Handful of parsley
1 tsp. thyme
6 whole cloves
1 bay leaf
A few whole
  peppercorns

Cover the chicken with water (about 3 liters/quarts) and add the rest of the ingredients. Bring to a boil and then simmer for about 3 hours or until water has been reduced to half. Strain broth and, when the broth is cool, put it in the refrigerator and keep it covered. You should have about 2 liters/quarts of broth. When cold the broth will be covered with fat, which you may easily remove before using.

Beef Broth

Ingredients:

2 kilos (4 lbs) soup meat
and bones
1 onion, cut up
2 cups (400 gr) cut up
tomatoes
3 ribs of celery
1 large carrot
Handful of parsley
1 tsp. thyme
1 bay leaf
6 whole cloves
A few peppercorns,
whole (black pepper)

You will have to ask your butcher for some soup meat and bones (only beef will do). Using 2 kilos (about 4.5 lbs) of soup meat and bones, cover with water (about 3 liters/quarts) and add:

Bring to a boil and simmer, partly covered, for about 6 hours. Check the volume of the water from time to time and top up if getting low. Cool down the broth uncovered and when cool cover and refrigerate. You should end up with about 2 liters/quarts of broth. When cold, skim the fat from the top of the soup before using.

Court Bouillon For Fish

Ingredients:

1¹/₂ kilo (3 lbs) fish rubbed with lemon juice
2 liters (quarts) water
1 bay leaf
A chopped carrot
3 ribs celery chopped
A small onion with 2 cloves
¹/₂ cup vinegar or 1 cup white wine
1 tsp salt
Handful of parsley

Court bouillon is a wonderful broth and may be used for any fish you wish to poach.

Add all ingredients, except for the fish, to the water and bring to a boil. Now add the fish and reduce the heat immediately. Simmer uncovered for 30 minutes, by which time the fish should be very tender. Drain and serve the fish, but reserve the liquids. You may use this court bouillon again, if you wish, when cooking any other kind of fish. It will keep for 3 or 4 days in the refrigerator.

Vegetable Broth

Ingredients:

3 large onions
4 carrots
1 clove garlic
2 large leeks (white part only)

1 bay leaf
Sprinkle of thyme
1/4 tsp ground coriander
1 clove
1/4 tsp. cayenne pepper
Salt and pepper to taste
Pinch of saffron

Chop the vegetables, place in soup pan and add and bring to boil 2 liters (2 quarts) water.

Add the herbs and spices to the pot. After bringing the water to a boil lower the heat. After about 40 minutes the broth will have reduced by half (approximately 1 liter or quart. Drain the broth and remove the vegetables.

Beverages

Iced Mind Tea For Summer

Ingredients:

Strong tea
1 cup water
1/2 cup sugar
1 lg bunch mint leaves

Make a strong pot of tea and let it sit until cool and then place in a tall pitcher.

In a saucepan boil the water with the sugar and a nice large bunch of mint leaves for 4 minutes. Strain this mixture before adding to the tea and then fill the pitcher to the top with water. Let cool and when ready to serve add some ice cubes to each glass.

Frappe

1 Serving

Ingredients:

1 large teaspoon instant
    coffee
Sugar to taste, usually
    equal to the amount
    of coffee
Water (at least 1/2 cup
    per person)
1/3 cup of milk
Lots of ice cubes

Put all ingredients in blender including ice cubes and blend for about 2 minutes. If making these in quantity make sure you do in small batches or else the coffee will overflow. Pour into tall glasses.

Special Times & Occasions

Breakfast or Brunch Menu

ORANGE JUICE OR MIMOSA OR BLOODY MARY

POTS OF COFFEE AND/OR TEA

FRESH OR TOASTED BREAD AND BUTTER

FLOSSY'S WESTERN OMELET

PANCAKES

EASY-TO-MAKE YOGURT COFFEE CAKE

FRESH FRUIT

Juice and/or Orange Juice Mimosa

Ingredients:

Orange juice
Champagne

Mimosa is a combination of orange juice and a splash of champagne.

Bloody Mary

Ingredients:

1 jigger of vodka
2 jiggers of tomato juice
1 tsp lemon juice
1 tsp Worcestershire
  sauce
2 drops hot pepper sauce
1/4 tsp salt

(This is just as delicious without vodka.)
For each serving, shake well and blend with some crushed ice.

Flossy's Western Omelet

Ingredients:

4 tbsp butter
1/2 cup diced ham
  (you may use veal or
  turkey ham)
4 slices of medium onion
8 strips green pepper
1 ripe tomato
8 eggs
Salt and pepper
Cheese (optional)

Using a sharp knife, cut the ham, onion and green pepper as tiny as possible.

It is important that the vegetables are finely diced. Beat the eggs in a bowl and put the butter in a pan large enough for the 8 beaten eggs. When the butter melts, add the onion, pepper and ham. Let them sauté in the pan until the onion and peppers are wilted and the ham is softened. Add the eggs; let them settle on top of the onions. When you feel that the bottom of the omelet is firm, turn the omelet over with a large spatula and cook until all of the egg is firm and well cooked. If the bottom is lightly browned, all the better. The success of this depends very much on how small the onion and peppers are minced. They should appear as specks rather than pieces.

This recipe is for 4 people and may be doubled for 8.

When the omelet is cooked some people add grated cheese on top.

Pancakes

Ingredients:

1 1/2 cups flour
1 tsp salt
3 tbsp sugar
1 tbsp baking powder
2 beaten eggs
3 tbsp melted butter
1 1/4 cups milk

Mix the dry ingredients (flour, salt, sugar & baking powder) and then make a well in the center of the flour mixture so that the center is hollow. Mix the wet ingredients (eggs, butter & milk) together until of a yogurt-like consistency. Pour this mixture into the hollow of the dry ingredients and mix together, but do not overbeat. If it is too thick, add more milk; if too thin, add a little more flour. Bring this bowl of batter and a large spoon to the stove and cook as below.

Place a flat griddle pan over an open medium flame and let it gradually get hot for about 5 minutes. Take a few drops of tap water in your fingers and throw the water into the pan. If the water sputters and bounces, the pan is ready. (If it just sits there, it is too cold. If the water disappears immediately then the pan is too hot.) When the pan is ready, dip a crumpled up piece of paper towel into the butter, using only a small amount. Smear the butter over the surface of the pan with the paper towel. Be careful, for the pan will be very hot. Now you will make a sample pancake. Put some batter into the center of the pan; when bubbles appear on the surface turn the pancake over and cook until golden on the other side. Taste it to see if it is cooked all the way through. If all is well then put butter in the pan again with a paper towel. Try making at least three pancakes together, spaced evenly over the hot pan. Or, if you wish, just make one big pancake that takes up most of the surface of the pan. Turn over when holes appear all over the pancake. The second side takes half the time of the first side. Continue to make pancakes until batter is finished. You may serve each batch of pancakes individually as you take them off the pan or you may stack the pancakes onto an oven pan in keep in warm a 100F (35 C) oven. In this way, everyone can eat the pancakes at the same time. They may cover the pancake with butter and then either honey or jam or maple syrup or anything else that appeals.

Easy-To-Make Yogurt Coffee Cake

Ingredients:

1 1/2 cups flour
1 cup sugar
1 tbsp baking powder
1/2 tsp baking soda
1/4 tsp salt
1 cup full-fat yogurt
2 eggs

Streusel:

6 tbsp flour
2 tbsp butter
5 tbsp sugar
1 tsp cinnamon

Preheat oven to 175 C (340 F).

Stir all of the dry ingredients together in a large bowl. In a separate bowl beat the yogurt and eggs together until homogenous. Gently combine the flour and yogurt mixtures and beat until smooth. Don't over-beat or the cake will be tough. Spread into buttered cake pan and cover with streusel.

Mix all ingredients together with your hands until crumbly. Dribble this mixture on top of the batter before baking the cake.

Bake in an ovenproof 22x22 cm or 9x9 inch square or round dish for about 20 minutes.

Fresh Fruit

Make an attractive dish of fruit of the season.

High Tea Menu

TEA SERVICE

CUCUMBER SANDWICHES

IRISH SODA BREAD

SCONES

LADY CAKE WITH LEMON ICING

Cucumber Sandwiches

Ingredients:

1 loaf of fresh sandwich
bread
Butter
1 or 2 small cucumbers
(if in Turkey try to find
the sweet, tiny
Çengelköy variety),
peeled and sliced very,
very thinly.
Salt

Remove the crust from the bread. Butter the bread and then place thin slices of cucumber on top; add some salt and then cover with another slice of buttered bread. Cut these sandwiches into four pieces and place on a silver or similar type tray. Make as many sandwiches as you need to serve your guests.

Irish Soda Bread

Ingredients:

2 cups flour
2 tsp baking powder
1 tsp baking soda
1/2 tsp salt
1 tbsp sugar
1/4 cup chilled butter
1 cup raisins
1 beaten egg
2/3 cup buttermilk or
 ayran (a mixture of
 water and plain
 yogurt)
Small amount of milk

Preheat oven to 175 C (340 F) degrees

Sift all dry ingredients into a large bowl. Mix carefully and then add 1/4 cup cold butter. With two knives cut the butter into the flour mixture until it has a course consistency. Add the raisins and then the beaten egg and the buttermilk. Knead everything together. If using a food processor, first blend the dry ingredients and then add the butter and blend until the butter becomes integrated into the dry ingredients. Don't over-mix as the butter pieces should be visible. Take out of the processor and add the egg, buttermilk and raisins. Stir well and knead briefly. Place in a buttered round baking pan about 20 cm (12 in.) across. Press down the dough and form into a round shape. Take a large knife and make a cut in half and then in half again. There should be four distinct sections. Brush the top with some milk and then bake for 35-40 minutes.

Scones

Ingredients:

1 3/4 cups flour
3 tsp baking powder
1 tbsp sugar
1/2 tsp salt
1/4 cup cold butter
2 eggs
1/2 cup heavy cream

Preheat oven to 220 C (425 F).

Put the flour, baking powder, sugar and salt into the bowl of your food processor. Mix together and add the butter. Keep processing until butter is the size of small peas. In a separate bowl beat the eggs (keep 2 tbsp aside to be used later). Remove flour mixture from the processor bowl and make a deep hole in the middle of the flour. Add the eggs and thick cream. Work very quickly and do not over mix when you combine everything together. Handle the dough as little as possible and put onto a lightly floured board. Pat lightly until it is about 2 cm (3/4 in.) thick. Cut with a knife into diamond shapes. Brush with the reserved beaten egg and sprinkle with sugar. Bake for about 15 minutes.

Lady Cake With Lemon Icing

Ingredients:

170 gm (6 oz. or 3/4 cup)
    butter
1 cup sugar
1/2 cup milk
13/4 cups sifted flour
2 tsp baking powder
1 tsp vanilla or l
    teaspoon brandy
3 egg whites

Lemon Icing:

2 cups powdered sugar
1/4 cup soft butter
1 or more large
    spoonfuls of thick
    cream
Grated rind of a lemon
    and the juice of the
    lemon

Preheat oven to 180 C (350 F) and grease a 25 cm (10) tube pan.

Cream the butter and sugar in a large mixing bowl and add the milk. Mix in the flour and baking powder and then add the vanilla or brandy. In another bowl beat 3 eggs whites by hand or with an electric mixer until stiff and dry and then fold into the cake batter very slowly so that the egg whites don't lose their shape.

Bake for 45 minutes and check to see if it is cooked by checking with a toothpick. When baked, let cool and then cover with the lemon icing.

Blend together the powdered sugar and the soft butter. When completely mixed add 1 or more large spoonfuls of thick cream. When correct consistency for icing, add the grated rind of a lemon and the juice of the lemon

Party Buffet

NORIKO'S BON FILE / BEEF TENDERLOIN

POTATO SALAD

CHICKEN SALAD

CHEESE AND COLD CUTS

SMOKED SALMON

TUNA PATE

BEAN AND TUNA SALAD

BREAD, CHEESE AND COLD CUTS

BARBEQUED WEINERS

LEMON SQUARES

Noriko's Bon File/ Beef Tenderloin

Ingredients:

1 whole or half
   tenderloin
Salt and pepper
A little oil to rub on
   meat

For a party of about 30 people you will need either a whole small beef tenderloin or half of a large one or approximately 2.5 lbs of very tender steak.

Because the cooked tenderloin is served cold it is very easy to cut into very thin slices. This recipe never fails if you follow instructions carefully.

Preheat oven to 250 C (480 F). Put the meat in a roasting pan, place in the oven and cook for 20 minutes, no longer. Turn off the oven and—very important— leave meat in the oven until the oven has completely cooled down. The meat should be perfect, brown outside and pink inside.

Potato Salad

Ingredients:

French Dressing:

1/2 tsp salt, ground
   pepper
1/4 cup vinegar
3/4 cup oil
1/2 tsp mustard

6 - 10 medium potatoes
   (6 medium potatoes
   will serve about 12
   people at a buffet.)
Chopped hard-boiled
   eggs, 2 at the most
1 grated onion
Sliced pickles of your
   choice
1 tbsp capers
Chopped celery leaves
1 tsp salt, or to taste
Paprika as an addition and
   also sprinkled on top
   when ready to serve
Some sprinkles of hot red
   pepper

(All ingredients available at large supermarkets.)

Place all French dressing ingredients in a jar and shake to mix.

This will give you 1 cup of French dressing.

For each kilo (2 lbs) of potatoes you will need 1/2 cup of the dressing. Boil the potatoes in their jackets until tender, peel the cooked potatoes as quickly as your hands can stand, dice and put into a large bowl. Immediately pour in the French dressing while still hot.

Add any, or all, of the accompanying ingredients. Mix well and refrigerate for at least an hour. One can add a little mayonnaise if you like, or some people like to add yogurt. Not too much, as it should not be overly creamy.

Chicken Salad

Ingredients:

2 cups cooked chicken.
1 cup chopped celery
1/2 cup blanched and
    chopped almonds
1/2 cup of French
    dressing (see recipe
    above).

Braise chicken breasts in some broth or water over low heat until thoroughly cooked. Pierce with a knife and make sure there is no pink in the center. After the chicken has cooked, dice and toss into the French dressing. When ready to serve add 1 cup of mayonnaise, salt and pepper, and garnish with pimento or olives.

Smoked Salmon

Ingredients:

As much salmon as
    needed
Juice of one lemon
Brown bread
Butter

Select a large tray; in the middle put slices of smoked salmon sprinkled with lemon juice and salt and pepper. Around the edge of the tray have slices of brown bread spread slightly with butter.

Tuna Pâté

Ingredients:

2 cans tuna fish (canned in olive oil and drained)
1 tbsp good quality olive oil
3 tbsp capers
8 tbsp softened butter
Sprinkle of paprika.

Place all ingredients in a food processor and run until completely mixed together and it has a creamy consistency. Either spread on crackers or else mold in center of a plate and put the crackers or, better still, some nice bread cut into squares. Sprinkle with paprika.

Bean and Tuna Salad

Ingredients:
850 ml canned (4 cups) canned white beans (drained in a strainer and rinsed with water)
A few chopped green, red or yellow peppers
Some minced garlic, 1 or 2 cloves
1 tsp oregano
2 tbsp chopped parsley
1 tbsp vinegar and the juice of 1/2 lemon
1/4 cup olive oil
Salt and pepper to taste
2 cans tuna fish, preferably the tuna canned with olive oil, drained

Mix all the ingredients together, chill, and place on a large platter garnished with tomatoes.

This recipe may be doubled if there is a large crowd.

Bread, Cheese and Cold Cuts

This section is entirely up to the cook. Select your favorite breads; slice thinly, put out a variety of the kind of cheeses you like best, and add if you wish some sliced meats like salami, etc.

Barbequed Cocktail Weiners

Ingredients:

About 40 (1 kilo or 2lbs)
good quality small
cocktail sausages
(about 7 cm/ 3 inches
long).

Put the sausages into an ovenproof casserole with 1 or 2 bottles of barbeque sauce (or use the directions at the end of this recipe). Put uncovered dish in the oven and bake for about $1/2$ hour or until the sausages are turning brown. Serve in the same dish and have several small forks nearby for people to use to put the hotdogs on their plates.

Barbeque Sauce:

1 small onion, chopped
1 tbsp oil
1/2 cup water
2 tbsp vinegar
1 tbsp Worcestershire
   type sauce
Juice of 1 lemon
2 tbsp brown sugar
1-2 tsp hot red pepper
   flakes
1 large bottle of ketchup
   (if you are using hot
   ketchup with flames
   on the bottle, then be
   careful to add less of
   the red pepper, or
   maybe none at all.
1/2 tsp salt
1 tbsp Dijon prepared
   mustard
Sprinkle of paprika

Sauté the onion in the oil in a large frying pan, add all of the ingredients and then simmer for 20 minutes. When cool, taste for more salt or pepper.

Lemon Squares

Ingredients:

1 cup flour (sifted)
1/4 cup powdered sugar
1/2 cup melted butter
(easily melted in the
microwave at high
heat for 2 minutes,
covered only with a
piece of paper towel)

1 cup sugar
2 beaten eggs
2 tbsp lemon juice
2 tsp grated lemon peel
1 1/2 tsp baking powder
Sprinkle of powdered
sugar

Preheat oven to 175 C (350 F).

1 square baking pan about 22 cm (9 inches)

Mix together the flour, powdered sugar and melted butter directly into the baking pan, press the mixture down so that it becomes like a pie crust. Bake this crust for 20 minutes in 175 C (350 F) oven.

After baking the crust, pour the remaining ingredients (except for powdered sugar) into the pan while crust is still warm, return pan to oven and bake for another 25 minutes. When cooked, place in the refrigerator. When ready, cut into 4 or 5 cm squares. You should have 16 squares.

Sprinkle the top of cooled squares with the powdered sugar.

Vegetarian Menu

CARROT SOUP

MY FATHER'S MACARONI AND CHEESE

MINT FRENCH DRESSING GREEN SALAD

LEMON DESSERT

Carrot Soup

Ingredients:

2 tbsp butter

Approximately 12 carrots (1 kilo / 2 lbs), peeled and sliced into rounds

1 large onion, minced

6 garlic cloves

1 tbsp cumin

1 tsp salt

3¹/₂ cups vegetable juice

1 tbsp lemon juice

¹/₄ tsp sugar

¹/₂ box thick cream

Chopped parsley

Heat butter in a large soup-sized pan. Add the carrots, onion, garlic and sauté until onion is soft, about 8 minutes. Add the vegetable broth Add the cumin and cover the pan and simmer about 30 minutes until carrots are soft. Puree soup in the pan with a hand blender until it is very smooth and then add lemon juice and sugar. Season to taste with salt and pepper. This can be made either on the day of serving or on the day before. When you are ready to serve, reheat the soup. In a small bowl whisk the thick cream until slightly thickened. Swirl the thick cream into the center of the bowl of soup and sprinkle on some parsley.

My Father's Macaroni and Cheese

This recipe serves 8 and it needs a large glass ovenproof dish. The recipe can be halved for 4 people. Even the halved recipe is quite substantial for 4 persons.

Ingredients:

A 500 gm (1 lb) package of the largest tubular pasta that you can find
2 cups (400-450gr) of chopped tomatoes. (You may also use the drained liquid to add to the sauce. In that case adjust the amount of milk.) (You may use canned whole tomatoes or blanched fresh and peeled tomatoes)
3 tbsp butter
3 tbsp flour
1 tsp salt and pepper
2½ cups milk – half canned evaporated milk and half whole milk. (If evaporated milk is not available use whole milk.)
400-500 gm (16-18 oz) extra sharp cheddar cheese.
Small amount of grated cheese for topping
Paprika

Cook the pasta in a large pot for about 13 minutes with salt added. Drain in a colander and place in a buttered oblong oven dish. Mix the drained tomatoes into the cooked pasta and with your hands distribute it well.

In a saucepan make a béchamel sauce by placing the butter in the pan and when melted add the flour; mix until completely combined and cook briefly. Add salt, a generous amount of pepper and the milk and tomato liquid. Stir together until a slightly thickened sauce is formed, stirring constantly, and little by little add the cheese which has been cut into small pieces. Continue stirring until cheese has melted and the sauce is thickened.

Pour this mixture over the pasta and the tomatoes, making sure that it reaches all corners of the dish and is distributed evenly. Sprinkle a little cheese on top if you like. Sprinkle with paprika. Bake in a 175 C (350 F) oven for 30 to 40 minutes. It should be beautifully browned and the sauce should be bubbling.

Minty Salad Dressing

Ingredients:

Selected salad greens

Dressing:

2 tbsp wine vinegar or
   lemon juice
1 tbsp Dijon mustard
6 tbsp olive oil
Sprinkle of salt and
   pepper
6 sprigs of fresh mint

Wash and dry all of the salad greens, tear to desired size and put into a deep salad bowl.

Put all dressing ingredients into a small jar and shake or mix in your food processor. Just before serving, pour the dressing over the leaves of salad, mix, and serve.

Lemon Dessert

Ingredients:

Crumb Crust:

15 graham crackers (petit
    buerre or digestive
    biscuits)
1/2 cup sugar
1/2 tsp cinnamon
1/4 cup melted butter

Filling:

3/4 cup sugar
1/4 cup cornstarch
Dash of salt
1 cup water
1/4 cup lemon juice
Finely grated rind of 1
    lemon
3 egg yolks
1 tbsp soft butter

Break up the biscuits and process in your food processor or blender. Otherwise, if doing this by hand, break up the biscuits with a rolling pin. Turn machine on and off to make crumbs. Add the sugar, cinnamon and melted butter. Process until blended together and remove from bowl and press into a 20 cm (8") flat ovenproof pie pan. Smooth the mixture with a large spoon in order to form a crust for your lemon pie. Let cool and bake in a 200 C (390 F) oven for 10 minutes.

Into food processor or blender or by mixer mix all remaining ingredients together. Empty into a saucepan and cook over low heat, stirring constantly, until thickened. Pour into the pre-cooked shell.

Cool well before slicing.

Family & Friends Dinner Menu

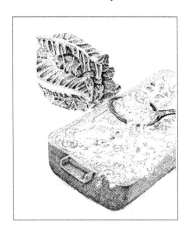

NORIKO'S FILLET OF SALMON

NEW POTATOES COOKED IN BUTTER

PEAS

GREEN SALAD WITH SLICED PEARS

GOLDEN CAKE WITH CHOCOLATE ICING

Noriko's Fillet of Salmon

Serves 8 people

Ingredients:

Salmon fillet pieces

2 tbsp soy sauce
1/2 cup brown sugar
2 tbsp olive oil
2 tbsp mustard
1 large handful of
   chopped dill or parsley

Have your fish seller cut enough pieces of salmon fillets for eight people. The salmon may be cooked with the skin on, or if you prefer, have the fish seller remove the skin from the fish.

Place salmon in ovenproof casserole, mix the soy sauce, brown sugar, olive oil, mustard and chopped dill or parsley in a small dish. Cover the salmon with this mixture and bake for 30 minutes at 175 C (350 F).

Small New Potatoes Cooked In Butter

Ingredients:

New potatoes -
   depending on size, at
   least 4 small, or 3
   slightly larger per
   person
4 tbsp butter
Salt and pepper

In a good frying pan with a substantial bottom and a good cover, melt the butter and then add the potatoes. Mix the butter and the potatoes very well and then cover and cook on the lowest heat possible for about 30-40 minutes. You must keep an eye on the potatoes to be sure they don't burn and you must turn them over and over frequently.

If time does not permit, you may place the potatoes and butter in a glass oven-proof casserole with a lid in the microwave. Mix and cook on highest heat for 5 minutes or so. If you have a lot of potatoes then you might have to cook them longer, 8 – 10 minutes. Both ways of cooking produce a pleasing texture.

Braised Peas With Lettuce In The French Style

Ingredients:

1/2 head of green lettuce
1/2 cup chicken broth
8 tbsp butter
1-2 tbsp sugar
2-3 sprigs of parsley
1/2 tsp salt
3 cups of frozen peas

Place the cleaned lettuce in the bottom of a saucepan. Pour in the broth; add 6 tbsp butter, sugar, parsley and salt. Bring to a boil and then stir in peas; cover the pan and bring back to the boil. Reduce heat and cook gently for about 15 minutes.

When the peas are finished the cooking liquid should have evaporated. Add the rest of the butter to the cooked peas and serve with the lettuce or, if you choose, serve the peas alone

Green Salad With Pears

Ingredients:

Assorted green and red
lettuce
2 ripe pears
3 tbsp olive oil
1 tbsp balsamic vinegar
2 tsp Dijon mustard
2 tsp honey

Place the washed and dried green and red leaves in a large salad bowl. Peel and slice the pears and place on top of the lettuce. In a small bowl mix the mustard and honey together, add the balsamic vinegar and mix well. Then add the olive oil and mix until the liquid forms a slightly thickened sauce. Pour over the lettuce.

Golden Cake With Chocolate Icing

Ingredients:

2 cups flour
2 tsp baking powder
1/4 teaspoon salt
1 cup sugar
3 eggs
1 tsp vanilla
3/4 cup of milk

Sift the flour, baking powder and salt and put in bowl. In another bowl cream the remaining ingredients, except milk, until soft.

Mix together the flour and butter mixture and then add the milk.

Stir the batter until smooth and pour into a greased 30 x 20 cm (12 x 8 inch) rectangular oven dish, a square pan or a round cake pan and bake for 25 minutes (if using a square or round pan you may want to slice the baked cake into two layers). After 20 minutes check the cake with a toothpick. Keep in the oven until completely baked and the toothpick comes out dry. The cake usually bakes in 25 minutes. Cool well before icing.

Chocolate Icing:

1 tbsp butter
120 gm (4 oz) bitter
    chocolate
6 tbsp thick cream
1 1/2 cups powdered
    sugar
1 tsp vanilla

Melt butter and chocolate in a heavy pan and watch very carefully so that it doesn't burn. When melted, beat in the thick cream. Add the powdered sugar little by little, beating after each addition until the icing is smooth. If the consistency is too thin add a little more of the powdered sugar. When icing is perfect add vanilla. Pour the icing over the cooled cake as soon as possible.

General European Menus

Central European Menu

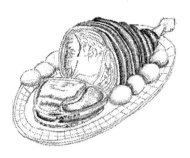

LIPTAUER CHEESE
HUNGARIAN ESTERHAZY STEAK
VIENNESE CUCUMBER SALAD
NOODLES WITH BUTTERED BREAD CRUMBS
SACHER TORTE

Liptauer Cheese

Ingredients:

2 packages (200 gm
    each) cream cheese
1/4 cup butter, soft
2 chopped anchovies or
    1 tsp anchovy paste
1/2 tsp chopped capers
2 tsp Dijon mustard
1 tsp caraway seeds
1/2 tsp salt
Dash of pepper
2 tbsp sweet paprika
2 tbsp chopped chives

Take all ingredients out of refrigerator at least one hour before preparing so they are at room temperature.

Mix the cream cheese and the butter with a fork in a bowl. When nicely blended add all other ingredients. Make sure the cheese is completely blended and then place in a small, deep bowl. Cover and chill in the refrigerator for several hours. When ready to serve, unmold the cheese onto a large attractive plate. Around it place slices of rye bread, flat bread or Melba toast.

Austrian Cucumber Salad

Ingredients:

3 large or 5-6 small
  cucumbers
3/4 tsp salt
1 clove garlic, mashed
1 tbsp olive oil
1/4 cup wine or white
  vinegar
1 tbsp water
2 tsp sugar
1/4 tsp paprika
Dash of pepper

The Austrians insist that cucumbers must be sliced by hand and absolutely not by machine. However you do it, make sure the cucumbers are uniformly thin.

Place the sliced cucumbers in a colander and add salt. Let stand abut 1/2 hour and the juice will have drained out. In separate bowl mix the drained cucumbers, oil, vinegar, water, garlic, sugar, paprika and pepper. Put in refrigerator for at least an hour before serving or for longer if possible.

Hungarian Esterhazy Steak

Ingredients:

1 kilo (2lbs) good quality
   lean beef steak
4 tbsp of oil
3 carrots, scraped and
   thinly sliced
2 small onions thinly
   sliced
Chopped celery
1 cup meat broth
1 tsp capers
1 tbsp flour
1/4 tsp salt and some
   pepper
Small dash of white wine
   or water
350 gr (1 1/2 cups)
   (12 oz) sour cream or
   whole yogurt mixed
   thoroughly with 2 tbsp
   flour
Paprika

Butter the insides of a baking dish; put aside.

Place meat on a plastic or wooden board and have a small amount of flour at hand which you will pound into the meat with a hammer or rolling pin. Pound the meat with flour on each side and then cut the steak into serving-size pieces. Give a final dusting of flour, salt and pepper.

Heat 3 tbsp of the oil in a pan. Add meat and slowly brown on all sides. Arrange meat in baking dish. In the same skillet cook the vegetables for about ten minutes. Spoon the vegetables over the meat and add 1 tsp capers. Now, add the remaining 1 tbsp of oil to the pan and blend in 1 tbsp flour and some salt and pepper. Add to this 1 cup of broth and bring to a boil. Add the wine and pour the thickened sauce over the meat in the baking dish. Cover dish with aluminum foil and bake at 175 C (340 F) for $1^1/2$ hours.

Remove foil gently and pour the yogurt mixture with the paprika over the meat and bake uncovered for about another half hour. Check to see if the meat is tender and if so take out of oven and serve in the baking dish.

Noodles With Buttered Bread Crumbs

Ingredients:

500gr / 1lb. wide noodles
1/3 cup melted butter
1 cup dry bread crumbs
1/2 tsp salt

Cook pasta as directed on the package.

In a frying pan, melt 1/3 cup butter; when melted add 1 cup dry bread crumbs and 1/2 tsp salt. Gently and slowly brown the bread crumbs until a dark golden color. Add to the cooked pasta, mixing in with vigor to make sure the crumbs on the bottom of the pan are fully incorporated into the noodles. Serve while hot.

Sacher Torte

Ingredients:

2/3 cup butter
3/4 cup sugar
8 yellow egg yolks
6 oz. semisweet
   chocolate, melted and
   cooled
10 egg whites
1 cup sifted flour
Good quality apricot jam
Chocolate Glaze

Chocolate glaze:

6-7 oz. bitter chocolate
1 tbsp butter
1 cup sugar
1/3 cup coffee or water

(Preheat oven to 175 C (340 F) and have ready a round cake pan, preferably spring-form, about 22 cm/9 inches round. Butter the pan before adding batter.)

Have the butter at room temperature so that it is quite soft. Put the butter and half of the sugar into your food processor, blender or mixer and process until the mixture is quite fluffy, then beat egg yolks very well with a mixer and then add the chocolate. In another bowl put all the egg whites and remaining sugar and beat with a mixer until the eggs stand up in sharp peaks. Add the egg whites and the flour alternately to the other ingredients. Fold in the egg whites carefully, with about four strokes. This method keeps the cake very light. When finished there should be some egg whites still visible. Pour the batter into the pan and bake for about 1 1/4 hours. You can tell that it is done when the batter shrinks away from the sides of the pan. Let cool and then carefully remove from the pan. When ready, see if you can cut the cake in half horizontally. Spread some apricot jam over the bottom layer and then replace the top layer and cover with chocolate glaze.

Melt chocolate and butter separately in the microwave at medium heat for a few minutes. Keep an eye on it so that it just melts and doesn't burn. Alternatively one may melt the chocolate in a saucepan on the stove. Make the syrup in another pan adding sugar, butter and coffee. Cook slowly and let the syrup get very hot, stirring constantly, until the mixture coats the back of a spoon. That means it will not run off but remain on the spoon. Be careful, for this syrup gets very hot and could burn you if you don't take care. Pour the syrup into the chocolate, stirring like mad and, when ready, pour over the cake.

Northern European Menu

SWEDISH PICKLED BEET SALAD

BELGIAN CARBONNADE

HOT GERMAN POTATO SALAD

DANISH PANCAKE-PANDEKAGER

OLD EUROPEAN CHOCOLATE SPICE CAKE

Swedish Pickled Beet Salad

Ingredients:

1 kilo (2 lbs) beets, peeled of outer skin and tops
1/2 cup vinegar
1/2 cup beet juice from your saucepan
2 tbsp sugar
2 whole cloves
1/2 tsp salt
3 peppercorns
Bay leaf
1 sliced green pepper
1 sliced small onion
1/2 tsp horseradish (if possible, or grated radishes like yaban or kara turp.)
1 bunch of dill

Peel and boil the beets until tender. Save 1/2 cup beet juice.

In another saucepan heat the remaining ingredients until they boil. Add the hot ingredients to the sliced beets and place in a covered jar or refrigerator dish. Cool for at least 12 hours before serving. Serve them sliced on a serving plate garnished with dill.

Belgian Carbonnade

Ingredients:

2 kilos (4 lbs) contre-filet
   or good steak
2 tbsp butter
1 medium thinly sliced
   onion
2 cups flat beer,
   preferably dark
2 cloves garlic
1 tsp sugar
1 tsp salt
1 tsp rice vinegar

Cut good quality steaks in half and coat with seasoned flour on a tray. In a frying pan with a cover, sauté the onion in half the butter. Remove from pan. Melt the rest of the butter and brown meat on both sides. Add the beer and bring to a boil. Add the garlic, sugar and salt and the reserved onions. Cover the pan and simmer 2 - $2^1/2$ hours until meat is tender. There should be a nice gravy left in the pan. Be careful to cook the carbonnade very slowly on the lowest heat. Some people add a little vinegar at this point. Taste first and then decide.

Hot German Potato Salad

Ingredients:

9 potatoes, peeled
1/2 cup diced bacon or
  ham
3/4 cup onions, chopped
1 tbsp oil
2 tbsp flour
2 tbsp sugar
2 tsp salt
1/2 tsp either caraway,
  mustard or celery seed
Freshly ground pepper
1/2 cup water
1/3 cup white vinegar

Cook potatoes in boiling water until tender, about 1/2 hour. When cool enough to handle, peel and slice thin. Put aside. If you are using bacon, cook in a cool frying pan until brown and then crumble into small pieces. If using ham, dice the slices into small pieces. Sauté the chopped onions in the oil until golden. In a bowl mix together the flour, sugar, salt, seeds and pepper and let them join the onions. Cook and stir until bubbly and remove from heat. Stir water and vinegar into the pan and once more return to the stove and bring to a boil for a minute or so. Add to the potatoes along with the bacon or ham. The salad is meant to be eaten warm.

Danish Pancakes-Pandekager

Ingredients:

4 eggs, separated
4 cups flour
1 tsp salt
1/4 cup sugar
3/4 cup beer
2 cups milk
1 tbsp melted butter
Strawberry or apricot
   preserves

Beat egg whites until stiff in a clean bowl. In another bowl beat egg yolks until thick. Add flour and mix well. Add beer, milk, salt and butter and beat until smooth. Very gently fold in egg whites. Pour some batter into your preheated flat griddle pan which has been buttered slightly. Place about 1/4 cup batter in the middle of the pan you may turn pan from side to side the make the pancake larger. Keep making until you have used all the batter. Brown on both sides. Serve with preserves.

Old European Chocolate Spice Cake

Ingredients:

2¹/₃ cups flour
2 tsp baking powder
¹/₂ tsp ground cloves
1 tsp cinnamon
¹/₂ tsp ground nutmeg
¹/₂ cup butter (at room
   temperature)
1¹/₂ cups sugar
4 eggs
4 oz grated bitter
   chocolate
7/8 cup milk

Bake in a lightly buttered tube pan (Bundt pan) for about an hour at 175 C (340 F). Preheat oven.

Sift the flour, baking powder, cloves, cinnamon, and nutmeg into a bowl. In another bowl cream the butter and sugar and then mix in the eggs. Stir the flour mixture into the butter mixture with your mixer or by hand and add the chocolate. Add the milk gradually and mix until very smooth. (Most European cakes are stirred for a long time and this gives them a firmer texture.

Bake in a pre-heated oven. After 50 minutes check your cake to see if it is cooked. Use the toothpick method to see if it is dry inside.

Usually this cake is just dusted with some powdered sugar poured through a strainer and scattered over the cake.

French Menus

Casual French Menu

TOMATO BISQUE
FRENCH ROASTED LEG OF LAMB
OVEN-BAKED POTATOES
ZUCCHINI BORDELAISE
TOSSED GREEN SALAD
FRENCH APPLE DESSERT

Tomato Bisque

8 servings

Ingredients:

3 tbsp butter
2 coarsely chopped
  onions
2 cloves garlic
1¹/2 kilos (3 lbs) fresh
  ripe tomatoes, diced,
  or two cans of
  chopped tomatoes
1 tsp oregano
4 cups broth
¹/2 tsp rice
1 tsp salt
Freshly ground pepper
Garnish of parsley or dill

Melt half of the butter in a large pan; add onions and garlic. Sauté them briefly without browning. Add the chopped tomatoes, oregano, the broth, the rice, salt and pepper. Bring to a boil and then simmer for about half an hour. When cooked, add the rest of the butter and puree in the pan with a hand blender, or in small amounts in a table top blender. Serve hot and garnish with parsley or dill.

Roasted Leg of Lamb

Ingredients:

1 leg of lamb (about 1$1/2$
   to 2 kilos/ 4 lbs), bone in
$1/2$ tsp Dijon-type
   mustard
2 tbsp soy sauce
2 cloves of mashed garlic
1 tsp oregano
$1/4$ tsp ground ginger
2 tbsp olive oil

Mash all ingredients in a bowl and spread over the leg of lamb. Put lamb in an uncovered roasting pan and roast in oven at 175 C (340 F). For one kilo (2 lbs) the roast will take about an hour. For a leg of lamb that is larger adjust the time. The French like to eat lamb that is on the rare side.

Roasted Potatoes

Ingredients:

About 1 kilo new
  potatoes
1 tbsp olive oil
1 tsp salt and freshly
  ground pepper

Wash and cut the unpeeled potatoes in half. Place in an oven dish. Pour the olive oil over the potatoes and sprinkle with salt and pepper. Roast in oven along with lamb for about an hour. Test tenderness with tip of a sharp knife. They should be nice and brown.

Zucchini Bordelaise

Ingredients:

750-1000 gr (2 lbs) small
   zucchini
2 tbsp olive oil
1/2 tsp salt and a
   sprinkling of pepper
2 tbsp fresh bread
   crumbs
1 tbsp butter
1 or 2 green onions with
   tops
Chopped parsley

Wash and trim the zucchini and cut in crosswise slices. Heat the oil in a large frying pan and when it is hot add the zucchini and sauté over high heat for about five minutes. Add salt and pepper. When the zucchini is cooked to your taste, add the bread crumbs and butter to the pan. Cook until the crumbs start to brown; throw in the chopped onion. Serve at once with some chopped parsley on top.

Green Salad

Ingredients:

An assortment of green
or red salad leaves

Dressing:
1 tbsp balsamic vinegar
1 tbsp mustard (Dijon if
possible)
1 tbsp honey
3 tbsp olive oil

Wash and dry the salad leaves and tear into desired size. Shake all of the dressing ingredients in a small jar until smooth. When ready to serve, pour the dressing lightly over the leaves, toss and serve.

French Apple Dessert

Ingredients:

8 large apples
4 tbsp butter
2 tsp vanilla
1/2 cup sugar

Peel about 8 apples, cut into quarters and then halve all the quarters. Place a large lidded pan on top of the stove. Using medium heat, add the butter, let melt, and then mix in the pieces of apples with the vanilla and sugar. Place on the stove at the lowest heat possible. It should cook for about half an hour. Alternatively, this mixture may be put into a covered, glass dish and cooked in the microwave for about 5 minutes at full power.

French Country Menu

TONY'S PURSLANE OMELET

SOUP BONNE FEMME

CHICKEN WITH RED ONION SAUCE

PUREE OF CELERY ROOT AND APPLE

COUNTRY APPLE CAKE

Tony's Purslane Omelet

Ingredients:

24 purslane (semizotu)
    leaves
6 large eggs
1/3 tsp salt
1/4 tsp freshly ground
    pepper
2 tbsp butter

Wash and dry the purslane and cut with a scissors into shreds

Mix the eggs, pepper and salt in a bowl; stir in the purslane. Heat butter in a nice sized frying pan over high heat. When the foam begins to subside and the butter has the fragrance of a nut, pour in the egg mixture. Using a fork, move egg from side to side. Tilt the pan and let uncooked portion move under cooked portion. When the eggs are set, tilt the pan and roll the omelet onto a warm dish.

Soup Bonne Femme

Ingredients:

1 kilo (2.2 lbs) potatoes
5 carrots
4 large leeks
4 tbsp butter
2 liters/quarts water
Salt and pepper
Lump of sugar
250 gr. (8 oz) heavy
　cream
Finely chopped parsley

Melt the butter in a large soup pan; put in the cleaned and chopped leeks and diced carrots. Let them mingle with the hot butter and then add the peeled and roughly chopped potatoes. Add the water, some salt and pepper and a small lump of sugar. Cook until the potatoes are soft. Turn off heat. When cool enough take your hand blender and smooth out the soup. Add the thick cream and top with the parsley.

Chicken With Red Onion Sauce

Ingredients:

1 or 2 chickens
1 tsp salt and freshly
   ground pepper
2 tbsp butter or olive oil
1/2 cup diced ham or
   bacon
About 5 cups of chopped
   red onions
1/2 cup white wine or
   broth
1 tbsp chopped parsley

Depending on the number of guests you may cook one or two small chickens. You should have your butcher cut the chicken into four pieces. If you choose a large chicken be sure that it will fit into your covered pan. Check to see if the chicken fits in the pan properly; if not, then cut up the chicken into smaller pieces. Reduce the red onions to 3 cups if you choose to cook only one small chicken.

Dry the chicken with paper towels so that it will not stick to the pan. Sprinkle with salt and pepper. Heat oil in large pan with a lid, add chicken skin-side down and cook until browned, 3 minutes for each side. Add the ham and the 5 cups of red onions. Cover the pot and let flavors mingle for 5 minutes. Add wine or broth and bring to a boil, stir and cover tightly and cook over low heat for about 45 minutes. Let chicken sit for another 15 minutes with the lid on and the heat turned off. Remove the chicken from the pan and keep warm and covered. Now turn the heat up under your pan and boil down the mixture until it is thick and sauce-like. Taste and add salt or pepper if needed. Place chicken back in pan to mingle with the sauce and then serve with chopped parsley.

This is a delicious menu provided that the chicken does not overcook. Keep checking to see if it is fully cooked with no red or pink flesh. If it seems completely cooked to you than then stop cooking and remove from pan and briefly heat just before serving.

Puree of Celery Root and Apple

Ingredients:

About 750 gm celery
    root
1 liter/quart milk
1¹/2 kilos (3 lbs) apples
¹/3 cup thick cream
Salt and pepper

Peel the celery root and cut into pieces; simmer in a saucepan covered with the milk for about 10 minutes. Meanwhile core and peel the apples and slice them into eighths. Add them to the celery root and cook for another 10 minutes until tender. Drain into a colander. Put the celery root and apples into your food processor, blender, or use your electric mixer and work until smooth. Cool, cover and refrigerate until ready to serve. It may be reheated gently in the microwave for 3-4 minutes, on high heat.

Country Apple Cake

Ingredients:

6-7 peeled and sliced tart
   apples
2/3 cup sugar
Cinnamon and nutmeg
3 tbsp melted butter
1 tbsp flour

Batter:

1 cup sifted flour
1/2 cup sugar
2 tsp baking powder
1/4 tsp salt
2 egg yolks
1 tbsp melted butter
1/4 cup milk

Select a pan that is deep enough to hold the apples and the batter, about 22 cm (9 in) in width, and butter generously.

Place the apples in the buttered pan and sprinkle with the sugar, spices, melted butter and flour

If you are making the batter by hand then combine all the dry ingredients together in a bowl first and then whip in the egg, butter and milk and combine well. If you are using a food processor you may put everything together except for the flour which will be put in a the end and combined very briefly.

Pour the batter over the apple mixture and bake in a preheated oven at 220 C (375 F) for 30 minutes.

Mediterranean Menus

Italian Menu

FLAT PASTA WITH LEMON SAUCE
SEA BASS - SOUTHERN ITALIAN STYLE
ZUCCHINI SAUTEED WITH OREGANO
ITALIAN MIXED GREEN SALAD
FRESH STRAWBERRIES

Flat Pasta With
Lemon Sauce

Ingredients:

500 gm tagliatelle, or
similar type pasta
$1/2$ tsp salt
5 tbsp butter
1 cup of thick cream
2 or 3 freshly squeezed
lemons
Grated lemon peel of 4
lemons
Grated parmesan cheese

Choose a pan large enough to accommodate the pasta. Bring the water to a boil and cook the pasta for about seven minutes. Add some salt. You can tell when the pasta is cooked by observing that is has turned more white than yellow. Melt the butter and the cream on high heat in a saucepan. When the cream begins to boil, add the lemon juice and stir and then add the grated lemon peel. Continue stirring until cream is thickened. Remove from heat. Add the sauce to the cooked pasta. Transfer to a serving bowl and toss together, making sure the sauce is completely incorporated.

Sprinkle with freshly grated parmesan cheese.

Sea Bass - Southern Italian Style

4 servings

Ingredients:

1/4 cup olive oil
2 kilos (4.5 lbs) of sea bass fillets, or a large fillet per serving.
Cup of flour spread out on a tray
Fresh ground pepper and sprinkling of salt
1 chopped onion
1 rib of chopped celery
3 tbsp capers
1/3 cup good quality vinegar

Place oil in skillet and turn heat to medium high. Take the fish fillets and put on top of the flour in the tray. Turn over once to flour both sides and then put into the pan with the hot oil. Cook until browned on each side and place them on a platter. Add salt and pepper. Put the chopped onion in the skillet and lower the heat to medium. Cook the onion until it is golden, add the celery, and cook for a few minutes more. Add the capers and cook for 1/2 a minute. Pour the vinegar over the onions and cook for a few minutes until all the vinegar has evaporated. Gently place each fillet into the sauce in the skillet and coat with the sauce and then place on a serving plate.

Zucchini Sauteed With Oregano

Ingredients:

750 gm (1.5 lbs) small
 perfect zucchini
1/4 cup olive oil
2 – 3 cloves of garlic,
 chopped
Salt and pepper
Handful of oregano

Wash zucchini well with a vegetable brush and discard both ends. Slice into thin rounds and set aside. Choose a large pan or a wok that will accommodate all the zucchini. Add the oil and garlic and heat the pan to medium. When garlic becomes a golden shade, add the zucchini, some salt, some pepper, and the oregano. Turn heat up to medium-high and cook uncovered for about ten minutes until tender. Keep stirring the squash so that it cooks evenly. When ready pour into a serving dish.

Italian Mixed Green Salad

Ingredients:

2 or more heads of green
and red lettuce

Salad Dressing:

5 tbsp chopped parsley
8 flat anchovies
Salt and pepper
2 tbsp balsamic vinegar
6 tbsp olive oil
3 tbsp grated cheese

Mix all the salad dressing ingredients in a small jar. Place your washed and dried salad leaves in a bowl. Shake the dressing and pour over the mixed greens. Toss and serve at once.

Fresh Strawberries

Ingredients:

1 kilo (2 lbs) strawberries
1 cup sugar
2 tbsp balsamic vinegar
2 tbsp orange liqueur

Wash strawberries in cold water before removing the stems. After washing, let soak for a few minutes and then wash again. Drain in a colander.

Remove the stems and cut the strawberries in half and place in a bowl. Sprinkle the balsamic vinegar over the strawberries and leave for a half hour. Then, add all the sugar and mix thoroughly. Again, leave the fruit to sit for a half hour or so. The vinegar immediately ripens and softens the fruit. Add the orange liqueur just prior to serving.

Greek Menu

CHICKEN AVGOLEMONO SOUP

SOFRITO FROM CORFU

MASHED POTATOES

GREEK SALAD

FRUIT BOWL

(All recipes serve 8 and may be halved for 4.)

Chicken Avgolemono Soup

Ingredients:

Water
750 gm (1.5 lb) carrots
1 bay leaf
1 large chicken
750 gm (1.5 lbs) of leeks
A bunch of green onions
100 gm (3.5 oz.) rice
2 eggs, separated
Juice of 2 lemons
Salt and pepper

Clean and separately dice the carrots, leeks and green onions.

On high heat bring about $2^1/2$ liters (8 cups) of water to the boil; add the sliced carrots. Cook for about 10 minutes, turn heat down and add the whole chicken. Cover and simmer for $1/2$ hour and then add the leeks and green onions and simmer for another 20 minutes, covered.

Take the chicken out of the stock when cooked and put aside with the cooked vegetables. Into the broth add the rice, stir, and cook for about 10 minutes.

Now to thicken the soup, the most important part of the recipe! In a large bowl whisk the egg whites with a hand whisk or with an electric mixer until they are firm. Add a good portion of the soup, about $1/2$ cup, into the bowl in which the egg whites have been whisked. Add this small amount of hot soup slowly, little by little, and now add the lemon juice and finally the egg yolks, which have been beaten until smooth. Lower the heat under the soup and add the contents of the bowl into the pan of soup gently and mix until the broth thickens. At this point the soup may only simmer. Do not allow to boil as it will curdle. You may or may not want to put some chicken pieces and vegetables back into the soup. This is your choice. Some people serve the soup plain and then place pieces of chicken and the vegetables in the center of the table.

Sofrito From Corfu

Serves 8

Ingredients:

6 good quality slices of
  beef steaks
3 cloves of garlic
Two generous handfuls
  of chopped parsley
1/2 cup (110 ml) vinegar
3/4 cup water (170 ml)
1/4 cup red or white wine
Salt and pepper
2 tbsp olive oil
Flour

Place some flour on a tray and press the steaks into the flour and turn over, making sure they are floured on both sides. Meanwhile, heat the oil in a large covered skillet. When the oil is very hot add the steaks and brown on one side. Reverse the steaks and brown on the other side and throw the chopped garlic into the pan. Allow the garlic to color. Add the vinegar and then the wine and then add water to barely cover the steaks. Add one-half of the parsley. Bring the liquid to a boil and then cover and simmer at lowest heat possible for an hour. During the cooking time turn the steaks over and re-cover. After an hour check the steaks for tenderness. If they are soft, and if the liquid more than covers the meat, uncover and reduce liquid so that there will be a nice amount of gravy to cover the steaks. Put on serving dish and sprinkle with parsley. (Sofrito is almost always served with mashed potatoes.)

Mashed Potatoes

Ingredients:

Potatoes (select at least
  one potato per person)
4 tbsp butter
1/2 tsp salt
Sprinkle of pepper
Milk (start with 1/2 cup
  and add more if
  necessary)

Wash, peel and quarter potatoes and cook in a large pot with lots of water and salt. When tender, drain all water from the pot. If you are using an electric mixer with its own bowl, then place potatoes in the mixer bowl. If you are using a hand beater then leave the potatoes in the pot. Add butter and blend together with the potatoes with a mashed potato tool or a large fork. Now add the milk, little by little, using your electric mixer. The potatoes will be very stiff at first; just keep adding the milk and some more salt until the consistency is perfect and creamy. You must serve these right away. If you have to wait then place the potatoes in a covered glass dish and put into the microwave for 5 minutes or put on stove over very low heat for a few minutes.

Greek Salad

Ingredients:

Tomatoes
Peppers
Cucumbers
Black olives
Feta cheese
Olive oil
Lemon juice

Greek salad is very much like Turkish shepherd salad except in the Greek variety the ingredients are cut into larger ($1/2$ in) pieces and a good-sized piece of feta cheese is either served on top of the salad or diced and mixed into the salad.

A simple dressing made of a mixture of the olive oil and lemon juice is mixed into the salad before adding the cheese. Parsley is often sprinkled on top.

Fruit Bowl

Gather together as many types of ripe
fruit as you can, depending, of course,
upon the season. Peel the fruit and dice
into fairly small pieces. In winter I use
oranges, apples, pears, kiwi fruits, and
plums, and in summer there is an endless combination of wonderful fruit.
Place the cut fruit in a nice bowl, add
some sugar to taste, and if possible a
small amount of fruit-flavored liqueur.

Spanish Menu

GARLIC SOUP

GAZPACHO ANDALUZ FOR SUMMERTIME

ROAST SPRING LAMB MADRID SYTLE

POTATOES CASTILIAN STYLE

CREAMY ALMOND SALAD FROM VALENCIA

FLAN (Spanish Caramel Custard)

All recipes serve 8 people and may easily be halved to serve 4.

You should be aware that the Spanish always use large amounts of garlic in their recipes. You may use less garlic if you wish.

Garlic Soup

Ingredients:

4 tbsp olive oil
8 cloves garlic (finely
chopped)
8 slices bread (remove
crust and dice into
small pieces)
2 tbsp paprika
2 liters/quarts broth
1 tbsp cumin
A few strands of saffron
2 - 3 eggs

Heat oil in large pan; when hot add the garlic cloves and cook until they are golden on all sides. Put them aside. In the same oil fry the bread pieces slowly until golden on both sides. Put aside. In the same pan add the paprika; then add the broth, cumin and saffron. Cook for 5 minutes and then taste to see if it needs any salt. Beat two eggs in a separate bowl and then add to the hot broth, whipping them into the soup until well mixed. Arrange the bread pieces on top.

Gazpacho Cold Soup For Summer

Ingredients:

750 gm (1.5 cups) fresh summer tomatoes (chopped) or canned ripe tomatoes (or a combination of both)

1 medium green pepper, roughly chopped

1 small onion, chopped roughly

2 small cucumbers, peeled and cut into pieces

4 tbsp apple cider vinegar

Sprinkle of chopped parsley

$1/2$ tsp sugar

1 clove garlic

1 cup tomato juice

Ice

Add all of the above ingredients into your food processor or blender and blend until completely liquid. Pour into bowls and garnish with some cucumber slices. You may add some hot sauce or red pepper if you like this soup spicy.

Roast Lamb Madrid Style

Ingredients:

Leg of spring lamb
2 tbsp olive oil
Salt and pepper
1 tsp paprika
1 clove garlic, crushed
2 cups broth
2 more cloves garlic
3 large slices onion
1 bay leaf
2 sprigs parsley
2 tsp vinegar
Sprinkles of rosemary, oregano and cumin
Juice of 1 lemon

Be sure that you use a roasting pan that will comfortably hold the lamb and also has enough space for a cup of broth.

Preheat oven to 220 C (425 F). Rub the lamb with the oil, then sprinkle with salt, pepper and paprika. Rub the crushed garlic into the lamb. Roast the lamb at high temperature (220 C) for 15 minutes. In the meanwhile, place all the remaining ingredients into a saucepan. Bring this mixture to a boil and let it remain on the heat for a few minutes. Reduce the oven heat to 175 C (350 F) degrees. Pour about half a glass of the boiling broth over the meat; baste the roast to keep moist. You must peek to see how quickly the broth is evaporating and then replenish with more hot broth every time the broth seems low. Make sure you use all the hot broth, and replace with hot water if the broth runs out. Cooking time depends on the weight of your leg of lamb; the rule is usually one hour per kilo (2 lbs). Take the lamb out of the oven and let it rest for 10 minutes before you slice and serve.

Castilian Potatoes

Ingredients:

6 tbsp olive oil
1 large minced onion
2 cloves garlic, minced
6 large potatoes, peeled
   & cubed
2 tbsp flour
2 tsp paprika
Salt and pepper
1 tsp oregano
Boiling water or broth to
   cover the potatoes

Heat the oil in a large pan. Make sure you use a pan that has a cover. When the oil is hot, gently cook the onion and garlic until wilted. Add the potato cubes and sauté until all the potatoes are thoroughly mixed with the onion. Sprinkle in the flour and paprika, stirring to coat the potatoes. Cover the potatoes with hot water or broth. Be careful not to add too much water; just barely cover the potatoes. Add salt, pepper and oregano and cook, covered, until potatoes are tender and most of the liquid absorbed; this should take about 20 minutes at medium heat. Be sure to turn several times while cooking.

Creamy Almond Green Salad

Ingredients:

Fresh lettuce leaves in
  any combination
1/4 cup blanched almonds
  (chopped)
2 cloves garlic, chopped
1/2 cup good quality
  olive oil
2 tbsp vinegar
2 tbsp lemon juice
Salt and freshly ground
  pepper to season

Grind the almonds with the garlic in a food processor or blender. Slowly, pour in the oil, then add the vinegar, lemon juice, salt and pepper. Beat until creamy and smooth. Pour over crisp, mixed green lettuce.

Flan

You will need a metal or ovenproof glass mold or round cake pan.
This pan may or may not have a hole in the middle,
and should be no more than 10 cm (4 inches) high.

For the caramel sauce:

1/2 cup sugar
1/4 cup water

First prepare the caramel sauce: Put the sugar and water in a heavy frying pan over a high flame, and melt until the sugar and water turn into a golden brown sauce. Keep stirring and don't leave the stove. It takes longer than you expect. Keep stirring and don't be distracted. Be careful to wear oven gloves or some protection from the sauce which is extremely hot. Be careful not to splash as the hot caramel can give a nasty burn. Don't let the sauce burn but keep on a high heat and stir constantly until golden brown. Pour into mold immediately and set aside.

2 cups milk, heated until very hot
1 tsp vanilla
3 eggs
1/2 cup sugar

Now make the main part of the dessert. In a saucepan scald the milk and vanilla. In a food processor beat the eggs with the sugar. When milk is very hot add to this mixture and mix. When all are combined, pour the milk and egg mixture into the mold. Place the mold in a pan that is larger than the mold—I use my roasting pan—and pour boiling water into the lower pan and let the water come up to about 3 cm (2 inches) below the top of the mold.

Bake at 175 C (350 F) degrees for about a half hour, but before taking from oven check to see that a knife inserted into the pudding comes out completely clean. Let the custard cool and then place in the refrigerator. When ready to serve the flan unmold it onto a dish large enough so that the caramel sauce won't overflow. Remove the flan with the help of a knife. Serve as you would a cake.

Moroccan Menu

CARROT AND CUMIN SALAD WITH CORIANDER
MOROCCAN LAMB TAGINE WITH PEARS
CAULIFLOWER WITH SAFFON,
PINE NUTS AND RAISINS
COUSCOUS OR PILAF
BANANAS WITH HONEY AND ALMONDS

Carrot and Cumin Salad

Ingredients:

500 gm (1 lb) carrots,
  cooked
1 tsp cumin
1 clove garlic
Juice of small lemon
$1/2$ tsp sugar
1 tbsp olive oil
Small amount of
  coriander leaves
Dash of salt

Wash and peel carrots and boil in salted water until tender. Drain when tender and slice into thin rounds. Mince garlic and add lemon juice, sugar, olive oil and cumin. Toss the carrots in this mixture and sprinkle with coriander leaves. The salad should be cooled before serving.

Moroccan Tagine With Lamb and Pears

Ingredients:

2 large onions, peeled and sliced

1 kg (2lbs) lamb from leg or shoulder cut into 4-cm (1.5 inch) chunks

2 pears, peeled, cored and cut into 4-cm (1.5 inch) chunks

$1/2$ cup raisins

$1/2$ cup slivered almonds

1 tbsp olive oil

1 tsp cumin

1 tsp ground coriander

1 tsp ground ginger

1 tsp cinnamon

1 tsp black pepper

1 tsp red pepper

Water to cover the meat

1 tsp salt

In large, covered saucepan gently fry the onions in the olive oil until soft; add the meat to the pan and cook until it changes color, and then add the spices. Add enough water to just cover the meat and add the salt. Put the lid on the pan.

Cover and simmer gently until the meat is tender, about $1^{1}/2$ -2 hours. Add the pears to the meat, together with the raisins and almonds, and cook for another $1/2$ hour. If I don't have enough pears, I use apples instead. Using half pears and half apples also works very well.

Cauliflower With Saffron, Pine Nuts and Raisins

Ingredients:

1 medium cauliflower, broken into small florets
2 tbsp olive oil
1 large onion, thinly sliced
Saffron, either powdered or in strands (if powdered, 2 envelopes in 4 tbsp hot water and if strands, place several in 4 tbsp boiling water)
3 tbsp toasted pine nuts
75 gm (2.5 oz or 1/2 cup) raisins, soaked in warm water
Salt and pepper

In a large pan bring water to boil, add a little salt, and when boiling add the cauliflower. Cover the pan and bring the water to the boil again. Cook for no longer than 5 minutes and then drain into a colander.

Heat 2 tbsp oil in a heavy pan over high heat. When the oil is hot add the onion slices, stir well, reduce heat and cook for about 20 minutes until golden. Keep an eye on them so they don't burn. Remove onions from pan. Now add the remaining oil and when it is very hot add the cauliflower. Fry until the cauliflower takes on some color. Then add the saffron, the onion, pine nuts and the drained raisins. Mix well and cook for roughly 5 minutes until the saffron water has dried up. Season with salt and pepper.

Couscous

Couscous may be found in the pasta section of your market. If you follow the directions on the package it is easily made. If you can't find couscous then a plain pilaf would be best to accompany the tagine.

Bananas With Honey and Pine Nuts

(Serves 8) but can be halved for 4

Ingredients:

8 tbsp butter
8 bananas, cut in half
    length-wise
1 cup honey
6 tbsp warm water
1 tsp lemon juice
6 tbsp sweet wine or
    water
4 tbsp pine nuts

Melt the butter in a frying pan, add the bananas and cook until golden, turning only once. In a bowl mix together the honey, water and lemon juice. Add to bananas and cook for about a minute. Add the wine or water and cook 2 minutes more. Sprinkle with pine nuts and serve hot. As an extra treat serve this over vanilla ice cream.

Western Mediterranean Menu

SICILIAN PASTA WITH EGGPLANTS

MALTESE SCAMPI

SARDINIAN CAULIFLOWER

CORSICAN LAMB STEW WITH PEPPERS

SICILIAN ORANGE SALAD

SWEET MADE WITH FRESH FIGS

CRÈME A L'ORANGE

Sicilian Pasta With Eggplants

Ingredients:

1 package Italian penne pasta (500 gm/1 lb)
2 medium, long style eggplants
2 cloves garlic
1 small chopped onion
3 tbsp olive oil
2 tbsp chopped parsley
2 cups chopped tomatoes – or if tomatoes are in season, dice about 6 tomatoes
Some red pepper
1/3 cup bread crumbs
Salt

Cut the eggplants in half and then peel. Cut into small cubes. Salt and allow to rest for a while, then rinse and dry and fry in some oil. Drain the eggplants and dry on paper towels. In a saucepan, sauté the garlic and onion until they begin to turn golden. Add the parsley, tomatoes, red pepper and salt. Cook, uncovered, for about a half hour. Add the small pieces of eggplants and heat for a few minutes. Just before pouring over the cooked penne, add the bread crumbs and mix well.

Maltese Scampi

Ingredients:

- 1 kilo (2 lbs) of jumbo-size shrimp, peeled
- 1 package of frozen peas
- 4 chicken breasts, sliced in pieces the same size as the shrimp

Marinate shrimp and chicken for several hours in the refrigerator (See recipe below). When ready to cook, first sauté the chicken pieces in hot oil until cooked, about 5 minutes. In a separate large frying pan, heat oil until hot and sauté the shrimp in batches if there are too many to cook at the same time. Be careful not to crowd the shrimp in the pan. Sauté for about three minutes until shrimp turn a pink color. Turn over and fry the other side. Prepare the peas as directed on the package, add some butter to the peas, and then pour everything together in one bowl.

Shrimp and Chicken Marinade

Ingredients:

Juice of 1 lemon
3 tbsp olive oil
Parsley
Hot pepper flakes
1 tbsp soy

Mix all ingredients together for a marinade that may be used for a variety of chicken and shrimp menus.

Corsican Lamb
Stew With Peppers

Ingredients:

1¹/₂ kilos (3 lbs) lamb cut into ³/₄ inch sized pieces
3 tbsp olive oil
2 large onions, chopped
2 large green peppers, cored, seeded and sliced
2 cloves garlic, diced
2 cups chopped tomatoes
2 glasses wine or meat broth
1 bay leaf
2 tsp oregano
Salt and pepper

Heat oil in a nice sized casserole or large pan with a lid. Add the lamb and brown meat on all sides with high heat. Remove from pan and put aside. Lower heat and sauté onions and peppers until soft. Add the reserved meat to the pan and add the garlic, tomatoes, wine or broth and the oregano and bay leaf. Season with some salt and pepper. Bring to a boil and then turn down heat and simmer for about an hour or an hour and a half. Check from time to time to make sure it isn't too dry; if so, add some water. This recipe is very nice served with tiny new potatoes, which, if you like, may be scrubbed with their skins on and added to the stew ¹/₂ hour before completion.

Sicilian Orange Salad

Ingredients:

4 large juicy oranges
Tender center stalks of
  celery, about 4 small
  ribs
3 tbsp olive oil
1 tsp vinegar
4 or 5 chopped nuts of
  your choice - walnuts
  are very nice with this
  salad

Peel oranges completely and slice in 1 1/2 cm (1/2 inch) slices

Cut celery into small pieces. Mix the oil and vinegar and pour over the oranges and celery, season with a little salt and pepper, and sprinkle with the nuts.

Sweet Made From Figs

Ingredients:

6-8 ripe figs, unpeeled

Arrange the figs in a baking pan with enough water to cover the bottom of the figs.

Sprinkle the figs with about 1/3 cup of sugar.

Bake in a 175 C (350 F) degree oven for about a half hour.

Serve cold with cream.

Crème A L'Orange

Ingredients:

3 oz sugar
4 egg yolks
Juice of 4 oranges
The juice of 1 lemon and
   the grated lemon rind

Put all ingredients into a saucepan, mix together and cook slowly, like a pudding. When the pudding thickens pour into a dish and let cool. Garnish with slices of oranges.

Turkish Menu (Rakı Table)

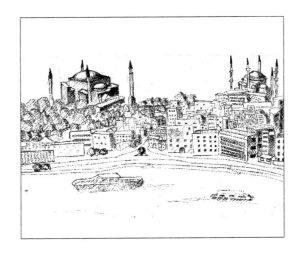

WALNUT CHEESE SPREAD

ALI'S MASHED POTATO SALAD

PIYAZ

FRIED ZUCCHINI AEGEAN STYLE

MARUL SALAD

SHRIMP SALAD

BAKED MÜCVER

MENEMEN

SMALL İZMİR KÖFTE WITH TOMATO SAUCE

Rakı Table

The Rakı Table is a happy occasion. Friends invite each other to their homes or to their favorite taverns - *meyhane* -to enjoy an evening of conversation, happy talk, and slow consumption of the alcohol, while all the while sampling food. The Rakı Table centers around the rakı, of course, that clear, anise-based alcohol the Turks call "lion's milk" (for its propensity to turn milky when diluted with water.

The rakı ın the *meyhane* ("house of drink") is accompanied by *meze*, numerous small dishes of delicious mixtures of vegetables, beans, fish, meat, spreads, savories and purees. All but the very stout-hearted drink their rakı diluted, generally at a ratio of about 1/3 rakı and 2/3 water, served with or without ice. The rakı is served and diluted in one tall and slim rakı glass, while an identical glass is filled with icy water. First come the cold meze - slices of melon, chunks of white cheese, and then all the cold dishes. An hour or so later, with the rakı still flowing, the waiters bring warm mezes—cheese and meat savories, sautéed mushrooms or other veggies, and a heaping dish of liver. For those who can manage, in another hour or so, the "main" meal comes - generally a platter of whichever fish is in season or a plate of grilled meat or meatballs. Whether the main meal is eaten or not, the evening finishes with a beautiful platter of peeled fruit.

People not only go to a *meyhane* for a Rakı Table, but it is also traditional to have one at the home as well, inviting good friends over an evening. There are literally scores of meze dishes that can be prepared and I have only presented a few here, but these are suitable for a fun and successful home Rakı night. Please feel free to substitute with any of your favorite dishes and salads, but do remember to provide the melon, cheese, plates of olives and – of course– a basket of fresh or toasted bread or rolls.

Walnut Cheese Spread

Ingredients:

250 gr (9 oz) white
    cheese
8 tbsp ayran or milk
1 cup walnuts
cayenne pepper
salt to taste
dash of paprika

Chop the walnuts in the food processor or blender with the cheese, ayran or milk, a dash of cayenne and some salt. You may add salt but be careful to taste the cheese first in case it is very salty. Blend to your satisfaction, taking care not to let the pieces of nuts get too small. When ready place the cheese spread in a bowl and sprinkle with paprika. (You may substitute other nuts if walnuts are not available, but I think the walnuts are the best.)

Ali's Mashed Potato Salad

Ingredients:

8 medium sized potatoes
3 cups water
1/4 cup olive oil
1 egg white
1 small grated onion
3 tbsp lemon juice
Salt to taste
1 cup finely chopped dill
10 black olives

Prepare the potatoes by peeling them and then slicing them into quarters. Place the washed potatoes into a saucepan and add 3 cups of cold water. Cook over high heat until potatoes are very tender and almost all of the water is absorbed. Mash at first with a potato masher, and if you have an electric hand beater this will make your job a little easier. While still hot add the oil and blend together. Continue to mash and add separately the egg white, onion and lemon juice. Still mashing, add the salt and dill. The potatoes should be smooth but not too thick. Put the salad into a glass dish that has a flat bottom and either rectangular or oval in shape. Add the olives by placing them in an interesting design on top. If the mixture seems too thick add a little more oil.

(Never put potatoes into a food processor)

Piyaz

Ingredients:

4 tbsp olive oil
4 tbsp lemon juice
1 tbsp wine vinegar
Salt and pepper to taste
1 can (800 gr-28.2 oz)
   white beans, drained
   (or dry beans cooked
   until soft but not
   mushy).
1/4 cup of chopped
   parsley
1/4 cup chopped dill
1/4 cup chopped fresh
   mint leaves
1 large onion cut in half
   lengthwise and sliced
   thinly
1 sliced tomato
1 sliced green pepper
10 black olives
2 quartered hard-boiled
   eggs (optional)

Use a bowl large enough to fit all the ingredients comfortably. First add the oil, vinegar, lemon juice salt and pepper to the bowl and mix well. Add the drained and refreshed beans into the salad dressing, mix well. Sprinkle the parsley, dill and mint on top. Lay the thinly sliced onions on top of the beans. Add the sliced tomato and green pepper, olives and eggs. Give a final toss of all the ingredients.

Fried Zucchini Aegean Style

Ingredients:

1 lb (about 5 or 6 small)
  zucchini
1 cup flour
1/2 cup (110 ml) beer
1/2 cup olive oil
Salt and pepper

Wash and dry the zucchini and cut off the top and bottom. Cut zucchini into lengthwise slices about 1/8 of an inch thick. Cover with flour, shake out and dip into beer. Fry in hot oil, turning over and cooking about three minutes on each side until the zucchini looks crispy. Serve on a large plate and put the yogurt sauce on the side.

Yogurt Sauce:

1/2 cup strained yogurt
2-3 cloves of garlic finely
  chopped

Combine the garlic with the thick yogurt, mix well and serve with the zucchini.

If you can't find strained yogurt, place a layer or two of cheesecloth into a strainer that is placed over a bowl. Add the yogurt and let the water drip into the dish below. This might take an hour or two and the final result is a very thick and delicious yogurt.

Romaine Lettuce Salad

Ingredients:

1 romaine lettuce
4 scallions, chopped
1/3 cup fresh mint leaves, chopped
3 tbsp olive oil
1 tbsp lemon juice
Salt and pepper

Strip the outer and tougher leaves off the lettuce and then slice into 1/2 inch strips across from the top to the bottom. You may wash the lettuce before cutting or after. I usually wash it after. Add salt and pepper and pour over the oil and lemon juice and mix well. If your head of lettuce is very large you might have to add more oil and lemon juice.

Shrimp Salad

Ingredients:

1/2 kilo (1 lb.) small
   shrimp
Olive oil, 3 tbsp
Lemon juice, 1 tbsp
Salt and pepper
Tomato, sliced
Parsley, 1/4 cup

You may purchase either raw or cooked shrimp. If raw, put shrimp into boiling salted water and cook until shrimp turns pink. Keep your eye on the shrimp so it does not overcook. Remove from water and let cool. Remove shells and toss with the other ingredients. It is traditional to place the shrimp in the center of the serving dish and garnish with the tomato and parsley. You may also add additional oil or lemon juice if you feel the need. Be sure of sprinkle with salt and pepper.

Baked Mücver

Ingredients:

6 small grated zucchini,
(1 lb, 500 gr)
3 eggs
6 scallions with green
tops, chopped
1/2 cup chopped dill
1/2 cup fresh mint leaves
1/2 cup chopped parsley
1 cup grated medium
hard cheese
1/2 cup broken up white
cheese (beyaz peynir
or feta)
11/2 cup flour
Salt and pepper
1/4 tsp cayenne pepper
4 tbsp. butter
10 black olives, optional

Preheat oven to 175 C (350 F)

After washing and drying the zucchini, grate coarsely into a bowl. (You may use the coarse grater of your food processor.) In a large bowl on top of the zucchini place the mixed eggs, scallions, dill, mint, parsley and both cheeses. Add flour a little at a time and mix well. You don't want the mixture to be too stiff so be careful with the flour, add 1 cup first and then when finished with all the ingredients add the rest of the flour. Do a little at a time so that the batter does not get too thick. Add the salt, pepper and cayenne. Grease a 22x22 cm (9 x 9 inch) oven dish with the butter. Dot the casserole with bits of butter on top. The olives are optional so if you are using them arrange in a design on top of the casserole. Bake for about 50 minutes until well browned. Cut into squares and serve hot or cold as part of your raki table.

Small İzmir Köfte
With Tomato Sauce

Ingredients:

500 gr (1 lb) lean ground
  beef
1 large chopped onion
2 or 3 slices white bread,
  put into water until
  soft and then
  squeezed dry
2 eggs
Salt and pepper to taste
3 tbsp chopped parsley
1 tbsp. chopped mint
  leaves or dried mint
2 tbsp ground cumin
1/3 cup flour
1/4 cup olive oil

In a bowl mix together the above ingredients, knead together and with wet hands shape the kofte into small meatballs and then flatten slightly to form an egg shape meatball. Roll in flour, heat oil in large frying pan over medium high heat and brown meatballs on both sides. You don't have to cook through because the kofte will continue to be cooked in the sauce.

Tomato sauce:

2 cans (400 gr, 14 oz)
    tomatoes
3 tbsp olive oil
5 cloves of garlic, peeled
    and smashed
1 1/2 tsp salt, sprinkle of
    pepper
Oregano, basil or any
    other herb, either
    fresh or dried, a few
    tablespoons
Pepper
1 tbsp cumin

You may use any tomato sauce you choose, either bottled or home made. This is a quick sauce I make in the microwave which is very successful. You might want to try it. Do not use only plain unflavored tomato sauce or tomato paste.)

Place everything together in a glass oven-proof bowl; no cover is needed.

Cook at high heat for 7 minutes, stir, and then cook for another 7 minutes.

Put the tomato sauce in the same saucepan as the kofte, stir the sauce and the meat together and cook gently in a covered saucepan on low heat for about 1/2 hour. Add some water if the sauce gets dry. Serve in small dishes; this kofte can be eaten hot or cold.

Menemen

Ingredients:

2 green peppers, chopped

3 tbsp olive oil

4 ripe tomatoes, chopped (Alternatively, you may use canned chopped tomatoes 400 gr. (2 cups) but it won't be as good.)

6 eggs

Salt and pepper

White cheese (beyaz peynir or feta) roughly about 150-200 gr. (6-8 oz.)

Menemen is usually made in a round, double handled frying pan. You may use your large omelet pan as the taste will be the same. Start by heating the oil in your pan until it is very hot. Add the green peppers and sauté until soft and just turning brown. Then add the tomatoes and let cook together until soft. Be careful not to burn. In a bowl, mix the eggs and then add the cheese which has been broken up into small pieces. Add to tomato mixture and quickly toss and turn until the mixture has become completely solid. Turn on to plates and eat immediately. It is probably better to salt at the table because of the saltiness of the cheese, which varies greatly.

Off-Continent Menus

American Menu

CALIFORNIA SALAD

MEAT LOAF

HOME-FRIED POTOTOES

MEXICAN CORN

BROWNIES

California Salad

(8 servings)

Ingredients:

Dressing:

5 tbsp oil
2 tbsp apple cider
   vinegar
1 tsp Dijon mustard
Salt and ground black
   pepper, to taste

4 ripe pears
Lemon juice
2 heads of mixed salad
   greens
Wedge of Roquefort or
   Blue Cheese
100-200 gm ($1/2$ cup)
   toasted and chopped
   hazelnuts

Put dressing ingredients into a small jar and shake. Peel, core and slice the pears and toss in a little lemon juice.

Put the cleaned and dried salad leaves into your salad bowl, crumble the cheese on top, scatter in the chopped hazelnuts, and add the pears. Pour the salad dressing over the leaves. Mix well and serve at once.

Meat Loaf

Ingredients:

750 gm (1.5 lbs) lean
    ground beef
1 egg
2 slices bread with crusts
    removed and soaked in
    water and then
    squeezed almost dry
cup barbeque sauce (or
    see recipe on page 51)
$1/2$ cup tomato paste
1 finely diced onion
A handful of chopped
    parsley
1 tsp salt
Freshly ground pepper
2 tsp Worcestershire
    sauce (optional)

Mix all ingredients together in a large bowl or mix together all the ingredients other than the meat and barbeque sauce and process in a food processor. Then add the ground beef and blend together very briefly, just to incorporate the meat with the sauce. Form a loaf shape and place in an oven pan or dish. Pour the barbeque sauce over the meat loaf.

Bake for one hour at 175 C/340 F. (You may want to place some aluminum foil underneath the meat in order to have an easier cleanup.)

Home-Fried Potatoes

(Serves 8)

Ingredients:

8 or 9 large potatoes,
thinly sliced
Olive oil to cover the
bottom of a large
frying pan
2 diced onions
Salt and pepper
Paprika

Heat the oil in a large frying pan that has a lid. When oil is hot, add both the sliced potatoes and the onion and sprinkle with salt and pepper. Cover the pan and put on the lowest heat possible. Cook for about an hour but keep turning and tossing the potatoes frequently. The secret of the dish is its being cooked for a long time over very low heat. Sprinkle with paprika when fully cooked.

Mexican Corn

Ingredients:

1 onion
3 tbsp butter
A few small, hot, green
    peppers, diced; if not
    available, normal
    green peppers with 1
    tsp hot red pepper
    flakes
2 cups diced tomatoes
    with juice
2 large cans corn (the
    type with no liquid
    added)
3/4 cup grated sharp
    cheese
1/2 tsp salt
Freshly ground pepper

Heat butter until hot but not burning.
Chop onion and add to hot butter along
with the green peppers. Cook until softened. Add the tomatoes and juice to the
pan and cook for about 15-20 minutes
until the liquid is reduced a bit. Add the
corn and cook again and let the sauce
thicken. Add the cheese and cook gently for about ten minutes. Add salt and
pepper.

Brownies

Ingredients:

1/2 cup butter
120 gm bitter chocolate

4 large eggs
1/4 tsp salt
2 cups sugar
1 tsp vanilla, or one small
   envelope of vanilla
   sugar mix.

1 cup flour

1 cup ground walnuts
   (optional)

Bake in a 22 cm (9 inch) square pan. The pan should be greased totally with margarine.

Melt butter and chocolate together over low heat or else melt in microwave in a glass dish, uncovered, for a minute or so until melted. It is important to let this mixture cool before using in the recipe.

Beat the eggs and salt and until they are light in color

Add sugar and vanilla and continue beating:

Now fold in the chocolate mixture.

Next fold into the bowl 1 cup flour.

If you wish you may add some walnuts at this point. Mix well and bake at 170 C (325 F) for about 25 minutes. Cut the brownies after they cool so as not to disturb the soft center.

Note: The eggs, salt, sugar, vanilla and the chocolate mixture may be mixed with a hand blender, blender or in the food processor. Just fold in the flour and do not overly beat. You should still see some white spots when you add the mixture to the baking pan.

Russian Menu

RUSSIAN CABBAGE BORSCH

PIROSHKI

BEEF STROGANOFF

PILAF

FRUIT KISSEL

In selecting the dishes for the Russian Menu, my mind went back to the old Rejans Restaurant in Istanbul. We had many happy times there and I decided to do some research and find the recipes for the dishes we most enjoyed at that time. Happily, the Rejans Restaurant still lives in the Olivo Passage. The desserts were all French then but I have given you a more humble dish.

Russian Cabbage Borsch

Recommendation: This can easily be done the day before.

Ingredients:

1¹/2 —2 kilos (3-4 lbs) soup meat
12 cups water
6 peppercorns
1 large bay leaf

First you must purchase some beef that is suitable for soup. Ask for advice from your butcher and then follow the following recipe.

Place the pieces of meat in a large pot with water, peppercorns and bay leaf. Bring to the boil, skim 2 times, then reduce heat, cover, and simmer for 2 hours or until the meat is tender. Remove the meat from the stock and put aside. Strain soup and remove any fat floating on top.

2 carrots, peeled and sliced
1 large onion
Salt (taste to see the saltiness of the broth)
1 cup full-fat plain yogurt into which 2 tbsp of flour has been added and fully mixed together
2 tbsp butter
2 tbsp flour
3 tbsp minced parsley or dill
1 small head of cabbage, shredded

Fry the carrots and onion gently in butter. When onions are golden sprinkle flour over them. Gradually stir in boiling broth. Add the shredded cabbage, cover the pan and simmer for about a half hour. Now add small pieces of the soup meat that you have put aside. Save some of the meat for the piroshki. Let soup cool a bit and then added the yogurt and flour mixture. Mix in but do not allow to come to a boil. Serve sprinkled with parsley or dill. Additional yogurt may be added at the table.

Pirozhky Made With Cream Cheese

This should make about 40 small pirozhki.

Ingredients:

250 gm butter
175 gm cream cheese or
   200 gm package of
   fresh white cheese.
1/4 tsp salt
230 gm (2 1/3 cups) flour
1 egg white (for
   brushing the dough;
   you may substitute
   milk if you like)

Meat filling for Piroshki:

2 medium onions,
   chopped
2 tbsp oil
Remaining meat from
   soup
Soup broth (depending
   on the amount of
   meat, you will only
   need enough to keep
   the mixture together)
Salt and pepper

Leave butter at room temperature for 1/2 hour before starting. Preheat oven to 175 C (350 F). Beat the butter with the cream cheese and salt. Add flour and knead rapidly. There should be enough flour to keep dough from sticking to your fingers. If necessary, add a little more flour. Form a ball, wrap in plastic wrap and chill in the refrigerator for about 15 to 20 minutes. When ready roll out quickly on a floured surface. Taking a normal size glass, cut rounds in the rolled-out dough. Stuff them with the following recipe and pinch the edges together with either fingers or a fork. Brush dough with the egg white or with the milk and bake for about a half hour or until golden brown in the hot oven.

Fry chopped onion in oil until golden. Put the meat in your food processor and run until the meat is thoroughly chopped. Add enough broth to moisten the filling and season with salt and pepper.

Beef Stroganoff

Ingredients:

1 – 1¹/₂ kilos (3 lbs) fillet mignon (bon file)
1 large onion
5 tbsp butter
1 kilo (2 lbs) mushrooms, brown colored if you can find them, then cleaned gently and sliced
1 tbsp flour
¹/₂ cup (112 gr) sour cream (to make a lighter dish substitute whole yogurt with 1 tbsp flour and mix thoroughly.
Salt and pepper

If the instructions are followed exactly, this is the most delicious beef stroganoff you will ever taste.

It is important that all ingredients be at room temperature, so take everything out of the refrigerator about 2-3 hours before cooking. During this time you may slice the onion very thinly and sauté at medium heat in 2 tbsp butter. In another pan place 2 tbsp butter and gently sauté the mushrooms. When both are soft, combine them, and then sprinkle with tbsp of flour and mix well. When the mixture has cooled add the yogurt and let this mixture rest for at least 2 hours or more. About an hour before serving, start cutting the meat. Cut the meat into thin strips lengthwise and then crosswise to make pieces 8 cm (3 inches) long. About 20 minutes before serving put the yogurt mixture on the stove and heat slowly and gently until hot. While it is reheating, fry the meat slices in another pan into which 1 or 2 tbsp of butter have been melted and is hot before adding the meat. Cook rapidly, turning the meat over and over, for 5 or so minutes or until the meat has stopped giving off juice. Remove from the flame and after it cools for a few minutes add to the sour cream or yogurt. If the gravy feels too thick, add some hot water; if too thin, add more sour cream.

In the real recipe for Beef Stroganoff sour cream is used instead of yogurt. Because sour cream is difficult to get in Turkey, I began using whole yogurt with flour mixed into it as a substitute and found it works very well.

Pilaf

(made in the microwave)

Ingredients:

6 tbsp butter
2 cups jasmine or long-
   grained rice
3 1/2 - 4 cups broth
1 tsp salt (depending on
   how salty the broth is)
Ground black pepper

In a large glass Pyrex dish place the butter and heat butter with highest microwave heat for 3 minutes. Stir in the rice and cook uncovered for 3 minutes. Add the broth, stir, and cover tightly. Cook at medium-high for 20 minutes. Uncover carefully because the dish and the rice will be very hot. You might prefer to do your own stove top recipe for pilaf.

Fruit Kissel

8 Servings

Ingredients:
For eight people you will need two 500 gm (1 lb) packages of frozen berries: sour cherries, strawberries, raspberries, etc.

1/2 cup sugar
2 tbsp cornstarch which has been diluted in 1/4 cup water

An easy-to-make and refreshing dessert.

Put fruit into a saucepan with 1 cup of boiling water and let it soften a bit in the hot water for 5 minutes.

To the pan of fruit add sugar and cornstarch and bring to boil and let cook for about 2 minutes. Pour into a bowl and cool in the refrigerator. Some whipped cream may be put on top.

You need to check on the sweetness. This dessert should always be on the tart side.

Keep in mind that if you use raspberries, they must be strained to remove the seeds, after they are cooked.

Asian Menus

Chinese Banquet

STIR-FRIED FRAGRANT CHICKEN

STIR-FRIED CURRY BEEF

STIR-FRIED MUSHROOMS

SWEET AND SOUR RED CABBAGE

CHILLED SWEET AND SOUR RED ONIONS

FRIED RICE

All of these recipes are delicious and you may select as many as you wish for a Chinese Banquet Table. As with Turkish *meze*, all the food is placed on the table at the same time. It would be easier to make these recipes with a very heavy wok.
See INTRODUCTION.

Chinese meals may be served in many different ways. When visiting Chinese friends I found that we always ate in the kitchen and the man or women who was cooking the meal was always at the stove. We ate course after course of Chinese food served right from the wok–everything very hot and very delicious. Not all of us are able to have dinner parties like this and so we have to make adjustments. In this particular banquet one could make the things served cold first, like the mushrooms, red cabbage and red onions. That would leave the chicken and the beef to be cooked closer to the time of the meal. The Chinese also serve plain rice with their meals, using leftover cold rice for fried rice the next day. Here I have put in a recipe for fried rice because I like it. So, you see, western adjustments have already been made. The other adjustment is to cook the chicken and the beef when convenient and then put the cooked food into covered glass dishes and microwave just before serving. In this way everything will be done by the time your guests arrive. This is your choice: either preparing the food before your guests arrive and sitting with your guests for the meal, or else cooking at the moment before your guests at the table. The choice is yours. It is also not necessary to make all of these dishes for your party.

Stir-Fried Chicken

(To ensure tender delicious chicken it must be treated before stir-frying. This very easy recipe appears at the end of this menu.)

Ingredients:

500 gm treated shredded chicken breast
2 - 4 tbsp oil
2 pieces of ginger
2 spring onions, finely chopped
2 cloves garlic

For 500 gm (1 lb) treated chicken pieces:

1/2 tsp salt
1 tbsp water or sweet wine
1 large egg white
1 tbsp corn flour
1 tbsp oil
1 pot of boiling water

About an hour before cooking in the wok make the following preparation:

Put the pieces of chicken in a bowl. Add 1/2 tsp salt and 1 tbsp water or sweet wine, and stir. Beat the egg white and add to chicken pieces, sprinkle on the cornstarch and mix well. Add the tbsp of oil and stir until smooth.

Let the chicken sit for about 1/2 hour before cooking. Cover but do not refrigerate. When ready, add 1 tbsp oil to the boiling water, scatter in the chicken pieces, and stir until chicken is all white, a few minutes. Pour the chicken into a strainer and put in a bowl and set aside.

Heat the oil until very hot in your wok. Place the ginger, spring onions and garlic on a small plate. Combine all the sauce ingredients and stir, making sure the sugar is dissolved.

Sauce:

1 tsp sugar
1/2 to 1 tsp red pepper
1/2 tsp black pepper
1 tbsp dark soy sauce
2 tsp rice vinegar
1 tsp oil with a little chili
   sauce added
1 tsp cornstarch dissolved
   in l tbsp water

Stir-Frying: Heat the wok or large heavy frying pan over highest heat until hot. Add the oil and heat until hot. Put in the onion, ginger and garlic and stir rapidly for a few seconds. Stir in chicken and stir quickly to blend with ingredients. Give the seasonings a big stir and pour in the sauce and stir intensely until the sauce covers the chicken. Pour into serving dish and eat while hot, if possible.

Stir-Fried Curry Beef

Ingredients:
500 gm tender steak
Only tender beef will do.
  The meat must be very
  soft in order to cook so
  quickly.)

Stir-frying:

3 tbsp oil
2-3 cloves garlic, finely
  chopped
1/2 cup minced onions
1 – 2 tbsp curry powder
1 1/2 cups diced green
  peppers
1 cup thinly sliced carrots
1 tbsp soy sauce
1 tsp sugar
1 cup water

Cut the meat into three strips, then crosswise into 1/8-inch-thick slices. Discard fat. Place the slices in a bowl, add soy sauce and sugar and toss to season well. Add the dissolved corn flour and oil and mix until smooth. Let stand for 15 minutes while you prepare vegetables. (Should you wish to do this in advance, cover, refrigerate and bring out a few minutes before cooking.) Chop the garlic, mince the onions, put green pepper into strips and peel and cut the carrots into thin slices. Place all ingredients on cutting board in separate piles.

For stir-frying:
  Heat wok or heavy pan over high heat until very hot. Add the 3 tbsp oil and let it get hot. Put in the garlic, toss around, add the onions, and stir around for about 1/2 a minute until they smell nice. Sprinkle in the curry powder and toss and mix thoroughly. Add the green pepper and carrots and stir in vigorously and let the vegetable sear in the curried

Sauce:

1 tbsp soy sauce
1/2 tsp sugar
1 tbsp corn flour
   dissolved in 1 tbsp
   water
1 tbsp oil

oil. Add the soy sauce and sugar and stir again. Add the water, even out the vegetables in the pan, cover and cook for 5 minutes with medium-high heat. Uncover after 5 minutes and add the meat and sauce, cover, and let steam for about 5 minutes. Uncover the pan, turn heat up to high and stir-fry vigorously for 1/2 a minute until sauce glazes everything evenly. Pour into a serving dish.

Stir-Fried Mushrooms

Ingredients:

500 gm fresh brown
mushrooms (otherwise,
white ones will do)
4 tbsp oil
1 – 1¹/₂ tsp salt (to taste)

Gently rub the mushrooms with a wet paper towel; trim off the ends of the stems. Slice them into thin slices and keep the stems attached. Heat the wok or large pan over high heat until hot. Add the oil and then turn heat to medium. Throw in the mushrooms and toss rapidly for 2 minutes, add the salt and stir a bit longer and pour into a serving dish. This may be served hot or cold. This can be done well ahead of the rest of the banquet.

Sweet and Sour Red Cabbage

Ingredients:

- 1 small head of red cabbage, about 750 gm (1.5 lbs)
- 3 tbsp oil
- 1 clove garlic, smashed, peeled and diced
- 1 tsp salt
- 2 tbsp apple cider vinegar
- 2 tbsp sugar
- 1/2 cup water
- 2 tbsp soy sauce
- 2 tsp sesame oil

Cut the stem off the cabbage, throw away tough outer leaves, quarter the cabbage and cut out the core. Shred the leaves of the four pieces into thin slices. Rinse them in a strainer of colander and shake dry.

Heat the wok or heavy pan over high heat until hot, then add the oil, and then heat for one minute. Press garlic into the oil, throw in the cabbage, and stir and toss rapidly until the shreds are shiny with the hot oil. Add the salt, stir, and then add the vinegar. The cabbage will change color to a brighter red; add the sugar and toss again. Pour in the water, even out the cabbage, cover and steam-cook for about 3 minutes but wait until you hear a crackling sound from the pan. Uncover, add the soy sauce and stir until there is no liquid left in the pan. Sprinkle in the sesame oil, turn over and over and then pour into a serving dish. This may be served hot or cold.

Chinese Fried Rice

Cooked plain rice: (This is the way the Chinese cook plain rice. You can follow your own recipe for making plain rice, if you wish.)

Ingredients:

1 cup jasmine rice
13/4 cups cold water

Wash rice in cold water. Pour 13/4 cups cold water into the pan with the rice and bring to a boil over medium heat. Let it boil for 1 minute and then turn heat to low; cover the pan tightly and simmer for 20 minutes. Don't remove cover, turn off the heat and let rice sit for up to 30 minutes. This makes 31/2 cups cooked rice. Uncover and let cool in refrigerator until you are ready to make the fried rice. The rice should be cold and so it can be done the day before, in the morning, or if you are like me and you forget to make it earlier, you will have to cool it quickly. Sometimes I put it in the freezer for a while.

Fried rice:

2 large eggs, beaten in a bowl
6 tbsp oil
3¹/2 cups cold rice
3-4 tbsp soy sauce
2-3 large green onions - cut into rounds including the green part

In a wok or a large frying pan, heat oil until very hot. Add 3 tbsp of the oil and heat for at least 45 seconds. Pour in the eggs and let them fluff up and move them around quickly and then as soon as they are cooked place on a dish near the stove. Add the remaining oil, add the rice and stir. With great vigor, quickly mix with a spatula until it is heated thoroughly and each grain of rice is covered with the oil. Add about a tbsp or more of soy sauce to the rice, mix, and put in the chopped green onions and the cooked eggs. Mix again and then put into a serving dish. If you can't serve right away, you can put the rice in a glass, covered dish and when ready put in the microwave and heat for a few minutes on high heat.

Sweet and Sour Red Onions

Ingredients:

5 medium
    (approximately 500 gm
    or 1 lb) red onions
2 tbsp oil
1 mashed clove of garlic
1/4 tsp salt

Sauce:

2 tbsp dark soy sauce
2 tbsp apple cider
    vinegar
2 tbsp sugar

Peel the onions. Cut each onion into halves and then cut into wedges, around four or five wedges per half onion; then separate the wedges into layers. Combine the sauce ingredients in a bowl and stir until the sugar is dissolved. Heat the wok or heavy pan over high heat until hot. Add the oil and heat until hot. Toss in the garlic and press into oil; add the onions and stir until they seem very shiny. Keep tossing for several minutes until they seem transparent and shiny. Sprinkle with salt and continue to stir. Add the sauce and as it sizzles stir onions again. Pour immediately into a dish. Let them cool for a few minutes, then cover and refrigerate until ready to serve.

Indian Menu

ROGAN JOSH

PILAF

CURRY PILAF

GLAZED CAULIFLOWER WITH GINGER

LENTILS WITH GARLIC BUTTER

YOGURT MIXTURE WITH BANANAS

Menu for 8 - 10 people

The Indian style of serving a meal differs from the European style of presenting each course separately. One should place all the food on the table at once and enjoy the mingling of the beautiful colors and exciting aromas.

Rogan Josh

Ingredients:

1¹/2 kilos boneless lamb cut into kebab-size pieces
4 tbsp butter mixed with light vegetable oil
1 tbsp minced garlic
2 tsp ground cumin
2 tsp ground cardamom
2 tsp garam masala
3/4 cup thick cream

Put all the ingredients of the marinade, except the butter, into a food processor or blender and run machine until all the ingredients are pureed.

Place the lamb in a large bowl; cover with the marinade and melted butter. Cover and let meat rest in marinade for 1/2 hour at room temperature or 2 hours in the refrigerator. Place the lamb and the marinade into a pan with a heavy bottom and one that can hold the meat comfortably. Cook over medium heat until mixture comes to a boil. Reduce heat and simmer, covered, until lamb is very tender, about 2¹/2 hours. Do stir the pan frequently during cooking so that the mixture does not stick to the bottom.

Marinade:

4 medium onions, peeled
  and quartered
2 tbsp chopped fresh
  ginger or powdered
  ginger
2 tbsp ground coriander
3 cups full-fat yogurt
  (low-fat yogurt will
  not work here)
1 tbsp salt
1/2 cup butter

Hear 4 tbsp butter in a small frying pan over high heat. When hot, add garlic, and stir for a few seconds. Add cumin, cardamom, and garam masala. Mix in and stir for a few seconds. The fragrance will be wonderful. Pour this mixture into the lamb, add the thick cream and stir to mix everything together. Let meat rest at room temperature for 2 hours. When ready to serve, check for salt, reheat until hot, and serve.

This whole recipe may be made a day in advance and refrigerated. The taste will even be better when the spices have had time to mature. One can always add another bit of butter sautéed along with the spices mentioned above to this dish just to make it more fragrant.

Pilaf Made in the Microwave

For 4 people

Ingredients:

3 tbsp butter
1 cup jasmine rice
1¹/₂ - 2 cups broth
1 small spoon salt
  (depending on how
  salty the broth is)
Ground black pepper

Heat butter with highest heat in microwave for 3 minutes. Stir in the rice and cook uncovered for 3 minutes. Add the broth, stir, and cover tightly with casserole top or with plastic wrap. Cook at high heat (800) for 15 minutes, or else medium heat (600) for 20 minutes. I prefer the 600 heat for pilaf. Uncover carefully because the dish and rice will be very hot.

For 8 people:
    4 tbsp butter, 2 cups rice, 3¹/₂ - 4 cups broth.
    Cook as above for 15-18 minutes.

Curried Pilaf Made in the Microwave

For 4 people - double ingredients for 8

Ingredients:

3 tbsp butter
1 large tbsp curry powder
1 chopped onion
2 tbsp raisins
2 tbsp pine nuts
3 cloves of garlic, smashed and peeled
1 cup basmati rice
1³/₄ cups broth

Heat butter in a large glass dish for 2 minutes at highest heat. Stir in curry powder, onions, raisins, pine nuts and garlic. Cook uncovered for 4 minutes at high heat. Add the rice and stir and cook uncovered for another 4 minutes. Pour broth over the rice and cover the dish with a glass top or plastic wrap and cook for 20 minutes on (600) heat. Remove from oven and let sit for about 5 minutes before undoing the cover.

Curried Pilaf Made in the Microwave

Version 2 (Serves 8)

Ingredients:

4 tbsp butter,
2 tbsp curry powder,
1 large chopped onion,
1/2 cup raisins and pine nuts
5 cloves of garlic.
2 cups rice
3 1/2 -4 cups broth

Cook as above, butter on high heat for 3 minutes, curry powder, etc. for 5 minutes. Add 2 cups rice and cook together for 4 minutes; stir in broth and cook for 20 minutes.

Glazed Cauliflower
With Ginger

Ingredients:

1 small head of
  cauliflower
4 tbsp oil
1 tsp cumin
1¹/₂ tbsp shredded fresh
  ginger root, or 1/12 tsp
  ground ginger
2 small green peppers
¹/₂ tsp turmeric
1 tsp salt
1 tsp lemon juice
Chopped coriander
  leaves or parsley
Hot water

Cauliflower should be separated into small florets. Wash and place them by your stove along with all the spices and $1/4$ cup of hot water. Heat 3 tbsp oil in large frying pan or wok. When hot add the ginger and green pepper, stir, then add turmeric and salt and follow with all the cauliflower. Stir rapidly to blend spices into all the cauliflower. Add hot water, lower the heat, and add just enough water to cover the cauliflower. Cover the pan and cook for 25 minutes until the cauliflower is tender and crisp. Stir once or twice while it cooks. When ready, increase heat to medium and stir-fry to evaporate any liquid in the pan and to brown the cauliflower. You may add another tbsp oil if the cauliflower seems dry. Add lemon juice and chopped coriander or parsley.

Lentils With Garlic Butter

Ingredients:

1 1/2 cups red lentils
3/4 tsp turmeric
2 tsp salt
5 tbsp sunflower oil
5-6 garlic cloves, peeled
and sliced

After washing the lentils, put them into a deep pot along with the turmeric and 5 cups of water. Bring liquid to boil and then reduce heat to low and simmer for 25-30 minutes. Stir from time to time. Remove from heat and the stir the lentils with a wire whisk or wooden spoon to smooth the puree. Stir in salt.

Heat the oil and when it is hot add the garlic slices and fry until garlic is golden colored, about 2 minutes. Pour this garlic butter over the puree. Stir to mix together and serve hot.

Sweet Banana and Yogurt Salad

Ingredients:

2 tbsp blanched almond slices

2 tbsp sultana raisins

2 cups plain yogurt (full-fat)

4 tbsp honey

1/4 tsp ground cardamom or nutmeg

1 medium ripe banana, peeled and thinly sliced

Put almonds and raisins in small bowl and cover with 1/2 cup boiling water. Soak for 15 minutes. Mix the drained almonds and raisins with the yogurt, honey and cardamom or nutmeg. Add banana slices and carefully mix ingredients. This is best served chilled. This is sort of an Indian *cacık*, but sweeter and it tastes wonderful with Indian food.

Japanese Menu

GRILLED TUNA SUKIYAKI

JAPANESE FISH CAKES

BEEF TERIYAKI

SAUTEED GREEN PEPPERS

JAPANESE RICE

APPLE AND SPINACH SALAD WITH SESAME SEEDS

MIXED PICKLES

Japanese Fish Cakes

This is a good dish if you have some leftover cooked salmon.
If you happen to have some salmon left from the NICE
MENU FOR FAMILY AND FRIENDS this is an ideal time
to make salmon cakes.

Ingredients:

225 gm cooked salmon
340 gm potatoes
1/2 inch slice fresh ginger
1 cup hot milk
Salt and pepper
1 small carrot
2 dried mushrooms, or 2
   large fresh mushrooms
1 egg
1/2 cup corn flour
Oil

Sauce Sanbaizu:

1/4 cup soy sauce
1/3 cup rice vinegar
1 tbsp sugar

Peel potatoes, boil and mash with the hot milk, salt, and pepper. Cook carrot along with the boiled potatoes and set aside. If using dried mushrooms, soften in cold water, drain and mince. If using fresh mushrooms, sauté in a little oil briefly in the same pan you will use to fry the cakes. Peel the ginger and mince. Add the chopped carrots, mushrooms, and ginger to the mashed potatoes; then add the flaked salmon and the beaten egg and a little salt. Mix together in a bowl with your hands and distribute the ingredients evenly. This mixture should be firm enough for you to handle and form cakes. In a tray put the corn flour and spread it around. With wet hands form cakes of the mixture and place them on top of the corn flour. Turn them over so that they are coated on both sides.

The size should be up to you, depending on how many fish cakes you wish to serve. Heat oil in frying pan until hot, gently add the salmon cakes and cook until brown on both sides. Serve with the sanbaizu sauce.

Grilled Tuna Sukiyaki

Ingredients:

4-6 tuna steaks ($1/2$ for
  each person)

Sauce:

4 tbsp dark soy sauce
1 tbsp saki or vodka
2 tbsp rice vinegar
1 piece of fresh ginger,
  about $1 1/2$ cm thick
1 clove garlic

Grate the ginger and garlic and mix with soy sauce, sake, and vinegar. Marinate the tuna steaks in this sauce for at least 15 minutes, turning them over once. Cook the tuna either on your outdoor grill or your kitchen oven grill (preheated) for five minutes on each side. Just before removing, brush the tuna with the marinade once more and let the marinade form a high glaze on the fish. The glaze gives the tuna a lovely shine.

Beef Teriyaki

Ingredients:

- 6-8 beef steaks (entrecote or filet mignon) (1 steak for each person)
- 5 tbsp rice vinegar
- 5 tbsp soy sauce
- 2 chopped garlic cloves
- Minced fresh ginger, about 2 teaspoons
- 1 tbsp oil

Make a marinade by mixing the soy sauce, vinegar, finely chopped garlic and ginger. Marinate the steaks in this mixture for at least a half hour. Heat oil in frying pan and when hot add the steaks, browning quickly on high heat. After you turn the steaks over pour the rest of the marinade over the meat and cook for 4 or 5 minutes more until meat has taken on a glazed appearance.

Japanese Rice

Ingredients:

2 cups rice (short-grained
    rice)
3 1/2 cups water

Put the rice and water together in a heavy-bottomed saucepan with a good fitting lid. First bring to the boil and then put on the lid, turn heat to low, and simmer and cook for 20 minutes. When ready turn on high heat for 20 seconds, leaving the lid on, and remove from the flame. Let stand at least 10 minutes before removing lid.

The Japanese thoroughly wash the rice in cold running water and then place the rice in a colander and let it sit for about an hour before cooking.

Sauteed Green Peppers

Ingredients:

12 – 15 small green
   peppers
2 tbsp oil
2 tbsp sesame oil
3 tbsp dark soy sauce
1 tsp sugar

Cut peppers into 4 pieces after removing tops and seeds. Heat oil in large frying pan, add the peppers, and sauté over the hot flame for 4-5 minutes. Add the soy sauce and sugar and continue to cook until tender. Add sesame oil after the pan is off the heat.

Apple and Spinach Salad
With Sesame Seeds

Ingredients:

500 gm fresh spinach
1 tsp salt
1 apple
3 tbsp soy sauce
3 tbsp sesame seeds
1 tbsp sugar

Bring a large pot of water to the boil, add the cleaned spinach and the salt, and let the water come to the boil again and cook for 1 or 2 minutes. Remove and drain in a colander. Press down on spinach to remove excess water. Peel apple and cut into small pieces. Allow to stand 5 minutes in salted cold water. Toast the sesame seeds in a dry frying pan and cook until they jump, stirring constantly. Mix the seeds with the soy sauce and sugar. Cut spinach into 3 cm lengths, drain the apples and add to the spinach. Pour the sesame seed dressing over the top and mix gently.

Mixed Pickles

Have a platter of mixed pickles on the table so that the guests may help themselves at any time during the meal. The Japanese love pickles.

Southeast Asian Menu

CUCUMBER SALAD

PHILIPPINE STYLE LAMB CASSEROLE

CHICKEN KEBABS WITH SPICY SATAY SAUCE OR
PEANUT SAUCE

STIR-FRIED ZUCCHINI WITH SESAME SEEDS

TROPICAL FRESH FRUIT SALAD

GINGER TEA

(All recipes serve 8 and may easily be halved for 4 servings)

Cucumber Salad

Ingredients:

400 gm (1 lb) cucumbers
8 tsp rice vinegar
4 tsp soy sauce
1 tsp sugar
4 tsp water
1 tsp sesame oil
200 gm (7 oz) small,
    cooked, peeled shrimp
    (optional)

Peel the cucumbers into very thin rounds, put slices in a bowl, add $1/2$ tsp salt and set aside for about a half hour. Pat dry with paper towels and place in a bowl. Add the vinegar dressing and the shrimp if using. Toss to mix and serve.

Stir-Fried Summer Squash or Zucchini With Sesame Seeds

Ingredients:

1 kilo (2 lbs) squash or
   zucchini
2 tsp salt
4 cloves garlic
1-2 spring onions
3 tbsp oil
1 tbsp sesame oil
3 tbsp roasted sesame
   seeds

Trim the squash and cut in half lengthways. Then turn on its sides and cut into 0.5 cm (0.2 inch) slices and put into a bowl. Sprinkle with $1^1/2$ tsp salt and leave aside for about a half hour. Drain and pat dry. While you wait, chop the garlic and slice the spring onion into very fine rounds. Set a wok or large frying pan over high heat with the oil; when it is hot put the sesame seeds into the oil and move around for a bit but don't let burn. Remove the seeds and let them drain on a paper towel. Add the garlic and stir until it begins to color. Add the squash and stir-fry for about 5 minutes until they are crisp but tender. Put on top of the squash the remaining salt, the onion and sesame oil. Stir once or twice and add the sesame seeds. This dish may be served either hot or cold.

Philippine Style Lamb Stew With Potatoes and Peppers

Ingredients:

1¹/₂ kilos (3lbs) lamb cut into cubes

4 tbsp white vinegar

2 tsp salt

Freshly ground pepper

1 medium onion, chopped fine

500 gm (1lb) potatoes, diced roughly

6 cloves garlic, smashed

5 tbsp olive oil

Stick of cinnamon or 2 tsp powdered cinnamon

2 bay leaves

2 generous tbsp tomato paste

2-3 large green or red peppers

Put cut-up meat in a bowl and add the vinegar, salt and pepper. Mix and put aside for 30-40 minutes. Using a strainer drain the meat into a bowl, save the juice, and dry the meat with paper towels. Heat the olive oil in a wok or heavy frying pan, and over high heat start to brown the meat in the same pan; this might take more than one time because of the volume of the meat. Make sure it is thoroughly browned. After all the meat is browned nicely, remove meat from the pan. In the same oil, sauté the onions and garlic and cook for about 2 minutes, scraping the pan as you turn the vegetables. Now return the meat to the pan, add juice from marinade, any juices from the standing meat and a generous amount of tomato paste. Stir and cook briefly, add 450 ml (2 cups) hot water and bring to a boil. Cover the pan, turn heat to low and cook for 15 minutes. In this interval, peel the potatoes and cut them into cubes. After the 15 minutes of cooking, add the potatoes to the pan along with the red pepper, the cinnamon and bay leaves. Then add the peppers which have been cut into thin strips. Cover the pan and cook for another one and a half hours until the meat is tender.

Chicken Kebabs With Spicy Satay Sauce

Ingredients:

450 gr (1lb) chicken.
Cut the chicken into 2.5 (1 inch) cm cubes (the thighs are the favored pieces for this kebab but if you only have breast meat that will do as well). At some butchers or supermarkets you will be able to get these chicken kebabs already prepared on wooden skewers. Think of roughly seven kebabs per person because they are small.

Marinade:

1 clove crushed garlic
1 tsp ground ginger
1/4 onion, diced small
4 tsp soy sauce
1 tbsp lemon juice

In a bowl add all the marinade ingredients; put in the chicken pieces and rub the marinade into the chicken. Cover and refrigerate for at least 2 and up to 24 hours. Preheat your grill, either indoor or outdoor. Thread about 7.5 cm of chicken pieces onto a skewer. On the grill place chicken about 10 cm (5 inches) from heat source. Grill for about 5 minutes on each side or until the meat is browned. When unable to use the grill for one reason or another I have actually cooked these kebabs in a frying pan. Place a little oil in a large frying pan, put in as many kebabs that will fit comfortably and fry first on high heat and then reduce heat and cook until browned and well-done. You might have to do this in batches if you have eight people to dinner.

If you are not able to grill the chicken you may fry them until brown on both sides in a little oil in a large frying pan. In this case, it is more convenient to have the chicken already on the shish. This is an emergency measure in case there is no possible way for you to grill

Satay sauce:

1 can of coconut milk
(stirred to blend
together), available at
supermarkets

3/4 cup roasted peanuts

Splash of rice vinegar

1 tbsp soy sauce

3 tbsp minced fresh ginger

3 tbsp brown sugar

1 hot red pepper or dried
red pepper

them. Still, it's better to fry them than to not have them at all. They are very good dipped into either sauce. Don't buy bottled *satay* sauce. Make the effort to make it yourself because it is so much better.

Satay Sauce

For both satay sauce and peanut sauce you may either use your food processor or your blender. The only difference is that with the blender you must start at the end of the recipe and put in all the liquids first, adding the nuts and ginger last. This applies to both sauces.

First put your peanuts in the food processor and let them pulverize. This will take a few minutes.

Combine the rest of the ingredients in a food processor and run until smooth. The sauce may be kept in the refrigerator for 5 - 6 days.

For final serving of this dish, place satay sauce on the side of the serving plate and use as dipping sauce for the chicken kebabs. This dish should be quite spicy.

Peanut sauce:

1/2 to 1 cup roasted peanuts
Slice of ginger, peeled and diced
1-2 tsp chili sauce
1/4 cup soy sauce
3 1/2 tsp sugar
3 1/2 tsp Worcestershire sauce
3 tbsp sesame oil
5 tbsp broth or water

Peanut Sauce

First put your roasted peanuts into your food processor and run until completely pulverized; this will take a couple of minutes. When the peanuts are ready add the other ingredients. When refrigerated, this sauce keeps fresh for 2 - 3 weeks.

Fresh Tropical Fruit Salad

Ingredients:

1 cut pineapple
2 bananas
2 mangos or papaya (If these fruits are not available choose fruits that are available, like apples, pears, grapes, water or any other melon, etc.)

Toss together all the fruit. Add some sugar in case the pineapple is too tart. Let sit for a while, so that a nice syrup will form. Mix the salad and serve. You may also add a few large spoons of a fruit liquor.

Ginger Tea

Ingredients:

2.5 cm cube of fresh ginger
4-5 tsp honey

Peel ginger and chop coarsely. Put it into a small pan with 1 liter/quart water and the honey. Bring to the boil, turn heat to low and simmer gently for 15 -20 minutes. Strain and serve.

THREE-WAY MIRROR:
ISTANBUL, ATHENS, ROME

by Michael Kuser

"As the Bosporus sweeps all before it down to the sea, always water but different water, so does the cast of characters in the city change over time, always people but different people."

This turn-of-the-millennium portrait weaves together three light-hearted tales of Rome, Athens and Istanbul. Here are the Colosseum, the Parthenon, and Hagia Sophia, yet the characters show sides of each city that the casual visitor would never see. Fascinating fun. A Polish musician teaches a Georgian refugee how to beg on the streets of Rome; a Russian barmaid ducks a police shootout in Athens; a Kyrgyz madman climbs trees to watch eagles fly over the Bosporus.

The magical blend of art and politics illustrates the clash of cultures in Europe, and its easy style lets you toss the heavy mantle of history in air like a scarf in the wind.

ISBN: 978-9944-424-72-1
2010, 388 pages

Çitlembik Publications

ISTANBUL'S BAZAAR QUARTER
Backstreet Walking Tours

by Ann Marie Mershon and
Edda Renker Weissenbacher

Istanbul teems with history, architecture, and culture. You'll discover them for yourself as you follow these routes through the seldom-explored streets around Istanbul's famous bazaars: The Grand Bazaar and the Egyptian Spice Bazaar. Edda Renker Weissenbacher has wandered the bazaar district for decades, amassing a wealth of knowledge about these fascinating back streets. Ann Marie Mershon's photos enhance the authors' detailed descriptions of over 80 enchanting sites along these self-guided walks. Follow one or all four—and become familiar with the city's historical hans, mosques, and bazaars. Prepare to be beguiled by your excursion into ancient Istanbul.

ISBN: 978-9944-424-59-2
2009, 182 pages

Çitlembik Publications

BYZANTINE ISTANBUL
A SELF-GUIDED TOUR

by Robert van den Graven

Istanbul's glorious history as Constantinople, capital of the Byzantine Empire for over one thousand years, comes alive through this guide to the city's many Byzantine sites. From the awe-inspiring domed nave of Hagia Sophia to the majestic remains of the fifth-century Theodosian walls, from the exquisite mosaics of Chora Church to dungeons and underground cisterns, from Greek Orthodox churches to sacred springs, the ten walking routes in this book take visitors through every layer of Istanbul's rich Byzantine past. Not just a guidebook, *Byzantine Istanbul* presents in-depth background on the history, culture, art, and religion of the Byzantines, while fascinating and entertaining historical anecdotes will introduce you to the figures and events that shaped the Byzantine era.

This updated and expanded second edition features new photos and all new maps; information on newly restored churches and recent archeological excavations of the Great Palace and the ancient Eleutherius Harbor; and a new walk along the seawalls by the Marmara Sea, making it the most comprehensive guide to Byzantine Istanbul available.

ISBN: 978-9944-424-51-6
2009, 118 pages

Çitlembik Publications

AN ONGOING AFFAIR
TURKEY & I

by Heath W. Lowry

"Hit [sic], don't forget, you are now one of us. There are things that you have seen and heard here in Bereketli that no one else need know about."

A two-year stint as a Peace Corps volunteer in a remote western Anatolian village during the early 1960s changed the course of Heath W. Lowry's life in a way he could never have imagined. Lowry's touching vignettes, reflecting both the high and low points of his time there, are by turn humorous and tragic and reflect his affection for the villagers who embraced him as one of their own. Tales of friendship, hospitality and humanity are juxtaposed against the harsh dramas and social mores of a traditional agrarian society of that period.

ISBN: 978-9944-424-53-0
2008, 200 pages

Çitlembik Publications